Maths

For the CEM (Durham University) test

The 11+ Study Book

and Parents' Guide

This book contains two pull-out sections:

A **Benchmark Test** at the front
A **Parents' Guide to 11+ Maths** at the back

1. $7 - 4.7 =$ (_____)

2. Round 12 853 to the nearest 1000.
   a 12 000 **b** 12 900 **c** 12 850 **d** 13 000 **e** 10 000 (_____)

3. Which of these numbers has 8 and 6 as factors?
   a 48 **b** 36 **c** 42 **d** 32 **e** 56 (_____)

4. Jason wrote down the number of siblings each person in his class had.

   0, 1, 3, 4, 3, 2, 3, 4, 0, 1, 2, 3, 0

   What is the mean number of siblings? (_____)

5. Which of these shapes is the same as shape **m**?

   m   **a**   **b**   **c**   **d**   **e** (_____)

6. Each side of a regular hexagon is 17 cm long.
   What is the perimeter of the hexagon? (_____ cm)

7. Which number could x represent?
   a 3 **b** 12 **c** 4 **d** 13 **e** 10 (_____)

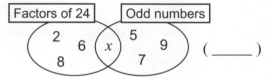

8. Phil has a jug which holds 1200 ml of water. He fills twenty-four
   10 ml test tubes from the jug. How much water is left in the jug? (_____ ml)

9. Jacques has three bananas for every two oranges in his fruit bowl.
   He has 12 bananas. How many oranges does he have? (_____)

10. It takes 30 seconds to pump 20 litres of petrol into a car.
    How long would it take to pump 60 litres into a car?
    a 1 minute and 45 seconds   **c** 1 minute and 50 seconds   **e** 3 minutes
    b 1 minute and 30 seconds   **d** 2 minutes and 30 seconds (_____)

11. $(5 + 72) \div 7 =$ (_____)

12. If $a = 6$ and $b = 4$, what is $4a + 5b$? (_____)

END OF TEST

/12

MHRDE1

1.   234 + 58 =   (_____)

2.   Which pair of numbers are both multiples of 9?
     a 63 and 56   **b** 78 and 92   **c** 54 and 66   **d** 45 and 72   **e** 81 and 68   (_____)

3.   23, 18, 13, 8, ____
     What is the next number in the sequence?
     a 2   **b** 3   **c** 1   **d** 0   **e** 4   (_____)

4.   84 ÷ 6 =   (_____)

5.   What is $^6/_{10}$ as a decimal?
     a 0.6   **b** 0.66   **c** 0.06   **d** 0.3   **e** 0.16   (_____)

6.   87 × 4 =   (_____)

7.   How many right angles does this shape have?   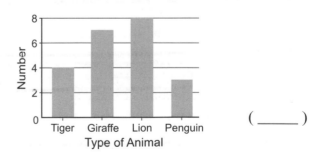   (_____)

8.   Olga ran a race which was 25 000 m.
     How many kilometres did she run?
     a 2.5 km   **b** 0.25 km   **c** 250 km   **d** 25 km   **e** 0.025 km   (_____)

9.   Andy is measuring the width of a table. He works out that the width of the
     table is equal to the length of eight 15 cm rulers. How wide is the table?   (_____ cm)

10. Class 4H went to the zoo and counted
     how many of each animal there were.

     They recorded their results in a bar chart.
     How many giraffes and lions were there
     altogether?   (_____)

11. $\frac{1}{3}$ of hexagon **m** is shaded. Which of these
     hexagons has the same amount shaded?

     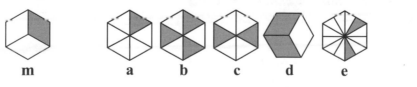

     m   **a**   **b**   **c**   **d**   **e**   (_____)

12. Jeanne arrives at hockey training at 5:35 pm. She plays hockey for 90 minutes.
     At what time does she finish playing hockey?
     a 6:55 pm   **b** 7:05 pm   **c** 7:15 pm   **d** 7:25 pm   **e** 7:45 pm   (_____)

/12

MHRDE1

11+ Maths — Benchmark Test

There are 36 questions in this test and it should take about 40 minutes. Write the answer to each question in the brackets at the end of the line. If there are a range of options, write the letter of the answer you have chosen. Use rough paper for your working.

Section One

1. $30 + 90 =$ (120)

2. $110 - 60 =$ (50)

3. $9 \times 7 =$ (___)

4. Round 544 to the nearest 10.
    a 540 **b** 550 **c** 600 **d** 500 **e** 545   (a)

5. What fraction of this shape is shaded?
    a $\frac{3}{4}$ **b** $\frac{1}{5}$ **c** $\frac{1}{4}$ **d** $\frac{1}{3}$ **e** $\frac{1}{6}$ (b)

6. 2, 6, 10, 14, __18__
    What is the next number in the sequence?   (18)

7. How many faces does this shape have?
    a 3 **b** 4 **c** 5 **d** 6 **e** 7 (c)

8. How many centimetres are there in 3 metres?
    a 100 **b** 30 **c** 130 **d** 300 **e** 3000   (e)

9. A box contains 72 bananas. The bananas are shared equally between 6 people. How many bananas does each person get?   (12)

10. Which of these clocks shows a quarter to 8?

    a **b** **c** **d** **e**   (e)

11. Emmy feeds her dog 200 g of dog food each day.
    How much food would she give her dog in 4 days?   (50 g)

12. Simon has 87 flowers in his garden. Simon's flowers are either red, blue or yellow. He has 29 red flowers and 34 blue flowers.
    How many yellow flowers does he have?   (130)

/12

MHRDE1

CGP

Maths

The 11+ Study Book

and Parents' Guide

For the CEM (Durham University) test

Practise • Prepare • Pass

Everything your child needs for 11+ success

CONTENTS

Section Four — Data Handling

Section Five — Shape and Space

Section Six — Units and Measures

Section Seven — Mixed Problems

Published by CGP

Editors:
Joe Brazier, Shaun Harrogate and Paul Jordin

With thanks to Sharon Keeley-Holden and Rachel Murray for the proofreading.

ISBN: 978 1 84762 560 1

Printed by Elanders Ltd, Newcastle upon Tyne.
Clipart from Corel®

Based on the classic CGP style created by Richard Parsons.

What's in the 11+

Make sure you've got your head around the basics of the 11+ before you begin.

The 11+ is an Admissions Test

1) The 11+ is a test used by <u>some schools</u> to help with their <u>selection process</u>.

2) You'll usually take it when you're in <u>Year 6</u>, at some point during the <u>autumn term</u>.

3) Schools <u>use the results</u> to decide who to accept. They might also use <u>other things</u> to help make up their mind, like information about <u>where you live</u>.

If you're unsure, ask your parents to check when you'll be taking your 11+ tests.

You'll be tested on a Mixture of Subjects

1) In your 11+, you'll be tested on <u>these subjects</u>:

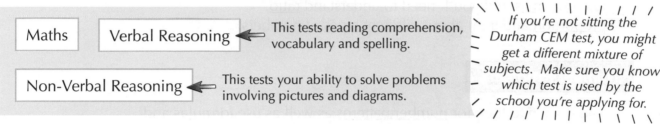

| Maths | Verbal Reasoning |
| Non-Verbal Reasoning |

This tests reading comprehension, vocabulary and spelling.

This tests your ability to solve problems involving pictures and diagrams.

If you're not sitting the Durham CEM test, you might get a different mixture of subjects. Make sure you know which test is used by the school you're applying for.

2) You'll probably sit <u>two 45 minute tests</u>, each made up of a mixture of subjects.

3) This book will help you with the <u>maths</u> part of the test.

Get to Know what Kinds of Questions you might get

The questions in your test could be either <u>multiple choice</u> or ones where you have to <u>write the answer</u> yourself.

Look out for the 'Tips and Tricks' boxes in this Study Book — they'll give you practical advice about the test.

Multiple Choice

1) For each question you'll be given some <u>options</u> — either on the <u>question paper</u>, or on a separate <u>answer sheet</u>.

2) You should draw a clear pencil <u>line</u> in the box next to the <u>option</u> that you think is <u>correct</u>.

Fill in the Blanks

To answer these questions, you'll have to <u>write numbers</u> in <u>boxes</u>. These will either be on the <u>question paper</u>, or on a separate <u>answer sheet</u>. Here's an example:

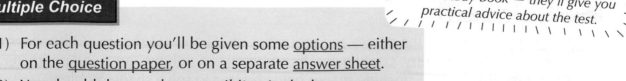

What is 34 × 40?   1 3 6 0

Just write the numbers neatly inside the boxes — you might not need to use them all.

What's in the Maths part of the 11+ Test

Here's a bit about the sorts of things you'll need to know for the maths part of the test.

Maths involves *Solving Number Problems*

1) You should have <u>covered</u> the maths topics that will be on the test <u>at school</u>.
2) We've grouped the topics that often come up into <u>seven sections</u> in this book.

Working with Numbers

You'll need to use <u>addition</u>, <u>subtraction</u>, <u>multiplication</u> or <u>division</u> to answer these questions (or all four to solve some mixed calculations). You'll need to use <u>place value</u> and <u>rounding</u> to solve number problems.

You might not be tested on questions from every topic in the real test.

Number Knowledge

You'll need to be able to work with <u>fractions</u>, <u>percentages</u> and <u>decimals</u> and you'll need to understand <u>ratio</u>, <u>proportion</u> and a bit about <u>different types</u> of numbers.

Number Problems

You'll need to look for <u>number patterns</u> as well as use <u>formulas</u> and <u>algebraic expressions</u>. You could be given <u>word problems</u> where you need to use information in the question to find the answer.

Data Handling

Some questions use <u>data</u> in <u>tables</u> and <u>graphs</u>. You'll need to be able to find information in a table and know how to read different types of graphs. You also need to be able to find the <u>mean</u> of a data set.

Shape and Space

You may be tested on the names and properties of <u>2D</u> and <u>3D shapes</u>. Other questions may ask about <u>symmetry</u>, <u>coordinates</u>, <u>transformations</u>, <u>volume</u>, <u>area</u> and <u>perimeter</u>. You might also have to imagine shapes being rotated to solve <u>shape problems</u>.

Units and Measures

You may be tested on <u>units</u> and <u>time</u>. You'll need to be able to <u>read scales</u> and <u>convert</u> between different units (e.g. mm and cm).

Mixed Problems

There might also be questions that cover <u>more than one</u> topic. For example, you may be given a question where you have to read a graph and do some calculations.

How to Prepare for the 11+

Give yourself a head start with your maths preparation — be organised and plan ahead.

Divide your Preparation into Stages

1) You should find a way to prepare for the 11+ that suits you. This may depend on how much time you have before the test. Here's a good way to plan your maths practice:

> Do the Benchmark Test at the front of this book. Ask an adult to mark it for you.
>
> ↓
>
> Learn strategies for answering different question types using this Study Book.
>
> ↓
>
> Do plenty of practice questions, concentrating on the question types you find tricky.
>
> ↓
>
> Sit some practice papers to prepare you for the real test.

2) When you first start answering 11+ maths questions, try to solve the questions without making any mistakes, rather than working quickly.

3) Once you feel confident about the questions, then you can build up your speed.

4) You can do this by asking an adult to time you as you answer a set of questions, or by seeing how many questions you can answer in a certain amount of time, e.g. 5 minutes. You can then try to beat your time or score.

5) As you get closer to the test day, work on getting a balance between speed and accuracy — that's what you're aiming for when you sit the real test.

There are Many Ways to Practise the Skills you Need

The best way to tackle 11+ maths is to do lots of practice. This isn't the only thing that will help though — there are other ways you can build up the skills you need for the test:

1) Practise your times tables with a friend by taking it in turns to test each other.

2) Divide up a cake, a pizza or a pie between a certain number of people. Work out what fraction each person is given.

3) Try drawing different shapes on a piece of paper. Use a small mirror to find lines of symmetry and work out what the shapes look like when they've been reflected.

4) Play games that involve counting like darts or MONOPOLY® to help you practise number calculations. You could also do activities like Sudoku to help you to develop your problem solving skills and play Battleships to practise using coordinates.

Place Value

Place value is about knowing the value of all the digits in a number.

Warm-Up Activity

Let's start with a quick warm-up.
Which of the following numbers is the biggest and which is the smallest?

10   10 000   100   1   1000

The **Value** of a **Digit** depends on its **Place** in a **Number**

Each Digit in a Whole Number has a different Value

1) This example shows what each of the digits are worth in a 7-digit number — **1 256 297**.

Millions	Hundreds of thousands	Tens of thousands	Thousands	Hundreds	Tens	Units
1	**2**	**5**	**6**	**2**	**9**	**7**
1 million, or 1 000 000.	2 hundred thousand, or 200 000.	5 tens of thousands, or 50 000.	6 thousand, or 6 000.	2 hundred, or 200.	9 tens, or 90.	7 units, or 7.

2) Each digit has the same value as 10 lots of the digit
to its right, e.g. 1 hundred is equal to 10 tens.

3) Whole numbers have a greater value when there are more digits,
e.g. 1 256 297 has a greater value than 256 297 because it has a millions digit.

4) When comparing whole numbers that have the same number of digits,
you need to look at the value of each digit starting from the left.
For example, 254 is greater than 249. They have the same number in the
hundreds column, but 254 has a greater number in the tens column than 249.

Each Digit in a Decimal Number has a different Value

1) This example shows you what each of the digits are worth in a decimal number — **1.365**.

Units	Decimal Point	Tenths	Hundredths	Thousandths
1	**.**	**3**	**6**	**5**
1 unit, or 1		3 tenths, 0.3 or $\frac{3}{10}$	6 hundredths, 0.06 or $\frac{6}{100}$	5 thousandths, 0.005 or $\frac{5}{1000}$

2) Each digit has the same value as 10 lots of the digit
to its right, e.g. 1 tenth is equal to 10 hundredths.

3) When comparing decimal numbers you need to look at each digit in turn. For example,
0.56 is greater than 0.53. They have the same number in the tenths column, but 0.56
has a greater number in the hundredths column than 0.53.

1

11+ Style Questions

Q What number is the arrow pointing to on this number line?

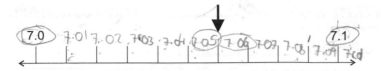

(7.0) 7.01 7.02 7.03 7.04 7.05 7.06 7.07 7.08 7.09 7.0 (7.1)

Method

1) Look at the <u>numbers</u> which are given and <u>how many points</u> there are on the number line.

   The answer is between 7.0 and 7.1, and there are ten points on the number line.
   The difference between 7.0 and 7.1 is one tenth, or 0.1. 0.1 is made up of ten hundredths,
   so each of the ten points on the number line is equal to one hundredth, or 0.01.

2) Count along the points to <u>where</u> the <u>arrow</u> is located on the number line.

   The arrow is pointing to the 6th point to the right of 7.0 on the number line, which means that this
   point is equal to 6 hundredths or 0.06. So the value of this point is 7 units and 6 hundredths, or 7.06.

Q Luca, Steve, Flo, Sue and Tom all drove one lap around a Go-Kart track. They put their results in a table.

Who drove the quickest?

Name	Time (seconds)
Luca	49.7
Steve	49.65
Flo	49.92
Sue	49.84
Tom	50.1

Method

1) To find out who drove the <u>quickest</u> you need to find the <u>shortest time</u>, which means that you're looking for the <u>lowest value number</u>.

   Look at the tens and the units of each driver's time. Tom's time is the slowest because 50 (which has 5 tens) is greater than 49 (which has 4 tens).

2) <u>Luca</u>, <u>Steve</u>, <u>Flo</u> and <u>Sue</u> all have the <u>same number</u> of <u>tens</u> and <u>units</u> in their time, <u>49</u>. So you then need to look at the <u>first decimal number</u> of their times.

   They each have a different value for the first decimal place. Steve has a lower number of tenths than the others, 6, so his time is quickest.

Practice Questions

1) Which of these is the smallest number?

   A 8.47   **B** 8.543   **C** 8.465   **D** 8.449   **E** 8.43

2) Which of these pairs of numbers are equally distant from 7?

   A 6.97 and 7.3   **B** 6.89 and 7.11   **C** 6.8 and 7.02   **D** 6.94 and 7.1   **E** 6.9 and 7.19

Rounding Up and Down

You guessed it — you can round numbers up or down to give an approximated value.

The **Number 5** is **Important** when you're **Rounding Numbers**

1) To round any number you need to follow a <u>simple rule</u>:

> • If the digit to the right of the one you're rounding is less than 5 then you round down.
> • If the digit to the right of the one you're rounding is 5 or more then you round up.

For example, to round <u>17 872</u> to the <u>nearest 100</u>, you need to round the digit in the <u>hundreds column</u>.

When rounding down, the digit you're rounding stays the same.

> **17 872** — The digit in the hundreds column is 8.

Now look at the digit to its <u>right</u>, in the <u>tens column</u>, to see whether you need to <u>round up</u> or <u>down</u>.

> **17 872** — The digit in the tens column is 7, so you round up 17 872 to 17 900.

2) You can use this method for rounding <u>decimals</u> too. For example, to round <u>1.428</u> to <u>one decimal place</u> (or the <u>nearest tenth</u>), you need to round the digit in the <u>tenths column</u>.

Rounding to two decimal places means rounding to the nearest hundredth. Three decimal places means to the nearest thousandth.

> **1.428** — The digit in the tenths column is 4.

3) To work out whether to <u>round</u> this digit <u>up</u> or <u>down</u> you need to look at the digit to its <u>right</u> — in the <u>hundredths column</u>.

> **1.428** — The digit in the hundredths column is 2, so you round down 1.428 to 1.4.

11+ Style Questions

> **Q** What is 46.98 rounded to one decimal place?

Method

1) Work out which <u>digit</u> you need to <u>round</u>.

   One decimal place is the first digit after the decimal point — 46.98.

2) Look at the <u>digit</u> to the <u>right</u> of the digit you need to round and work out whether you need to <u>round up</u> or <u>round down</u>.

   The digit to the right of the digit you need to round is 8 — 46.98.
   8 is more than 5 so you need to round up. Rounding up 9 tenths will give you 10 tenths, which is equal to 1 unit. This will increase the digit in the units column from 6 to 7 and leave 0 tenths. So 46.98 rounded to one decimal place is 47.0.

Q Which of these is 1500?

(handwritten: 1510)

(A)   1508 to the nearest 10   (D) *(1500)* 1498 to the nearest 10

B *(1400)* 1448 to the nearest 100   E *(2000)* 1504 to the nearest 1000

C *(1600)* 1562 to the nearest 100

Method

1) Look at <u>each option</u> one by one.

         A   1508: 0 is being rounded, 8 is more than 5 — 1508 rounds up to 1510 not 1500.

         B   1448: 4 is being rounded, 4 is less than 5 — 1448 rounds down to 1400 not 1500.

         C   1562: 5 is being rounded, 6 is more than 5 — 1562 rounds up to 1600 not 1500.

         D   1498: 9 is being rounded, 8 is more than 5 — 1498 rounds up to 1500.

         So the answer is D.

2) If you have time you can <u>check</u> your answer by looking at the <u>last option</u>.

         E   1504: 1 is being rounded, 5 is 5 or more — 1504 rounds up to 2000 not 1500.

(handwritten: 43,389   43.390 kg)

Q Round 43.389 kg to the nearest 10 grams.

A   50 kg   D   40 kg

B   43.4 kg   E   43.39 kg

C   43 kg

Method

1) You need to find <u>43.389 kg</u> to the <u>nearest 10 grams</u> —
it'll be <u>easier</u> to round this figure if you <u>convert</u> it into <u>grams</u>.

     A kilogram is the same as 1000 grams, so multiply 43.389 by 1000 43 389 kg is 43 389 g.

2) Work out which digit is in the <u>tens</u> column and look at the digit to its
<u>right</u> (in the <u>units</u> column) to see whether you need to <u>round up</u> or <u>down</u>.

     43 389: 8 is being rounded, 9 is more than 5 so 43 389 rounds up to 43 390.

     To convert this back into kilograms you just need to divide 43 390 by 1000.

     The answer is 43.39 kg — option <u>E</u>.

Practice Questions

(handwritten: 1+0 000)

1) Round 174 782 to the nearest ten thousand.

     A 174 800   **B** 180 000   **C** 170 800   (**D**) 170 000   **E** 175 000

(handwritten: 129456 m   129500)

2) What is 129.456 km rounded to the nearest 100 m?
Give your answer in km.

Addition

You've been adding numbers together for years. Here are a few examples of the sorts of questions you could get in the exam, and some methods you could use to answer them.

Warm-Up Activity

1) Ask someone else to join you and take it in turns to roll <u>three</u> dice.
2) <u>Add together</u> the three numbers. Give yourself 1 point if you score <u>8 or more</u>.
3) The first player to get <u>6 points</u> is the winner.

11+ Style Questions

> **Q** Marco has £4.13, Kyle has £3.42 and Janet has £8.70.
> How much money do they have in total?
>
> | | |
> |---|---|
> | A £15.95 | D £16.25 |
> | B £18.25 | E £14.25 |
> | C £17.85 | |

Quick Method

1) You can <u>estimate</u> the answer to the question by <u>rounding</u> the numbers to the nearest pound to make <u>more manageable</u> numbers.

> £4.13 is rounded down to £4.00   £3.42 is rounded down to £3.00   £8.70 is rounded up to £9.00

2) Add the <u>rounded numbers together</u> to estimate the answer.

> £4.00 + £3.00 + £9.00 = £16.00

3) The answer is <u>around</u> £16.00. Looking at the options, the answer could be <u>A</u> or <u>D</u>.

4) As you rounded <u>down</u> by 55p (13p + 42p) and you rounded <u>up</u> by 30p, your estimate will be <u>lower</u> than the actual answer. So, the <u>actual answer</u> must be £16.25 — option D.

Written Method

1) An <u>alternative</u> method is to add the three values together in <u>columns</u>.

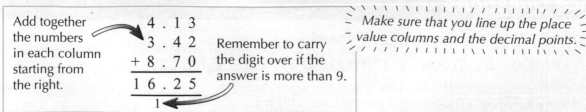

Add together the numbers in each column starting from the right.

$$\begin{array}{r} 4\,.\,1\,3 \\ 3\,.\,4\,2 \\ +\,8\,.\,7\,0 \\ \hline 1\,6\,.\,2\,5 \\ 1 \end{array}$$

Remember to carry the digit over if the answer is more than 9.

Make sure that you line up the place value columns and the decimal points.

2) This method gives you the <u>exact answer</u>, £16.25.

Q The table shows the amount of juice in litres sold by Cathy on her market stall over 8 weeks.

Work out the total amount of juice Cathy sold from week 3 to week 6.

Week	Amount of juice sold (l)	Week	Amount of juice sold (l)
1	43.71	5	46.30
2	46.18	6	59.12
3	82.63	7	21.14
4	34.18	8	63.94

Method

1) For this question there are <u>no options</u> to choose from.
   So you need to find the <u>exact answer</u> — you <u>can't</u> use rounding.

2) The question is asking for the total sales from <u>week 3</u> to <u>week 6</u>, so find the <u>data</u> you need in the <u>table</u>.

   > Week 3 = 82.63 litres   Week 5 = 46.30 litres
   > Week 4 = 34.18 litres   Week 6 = 59.12 litres

3) Arrange the four weekly values into <u>columns</u>.
   <u>Add together</u> the numbers in each column starting from the right.

Use the column method to find the exact answer.

```
    8 2 . 6 3
    3 4 . 1 8
    4 6 . 3 0
  + 5 9 . 1 2
  ─────────────
  2 2 2 . 2 3
    2 1   1
```

4) The total amount of juice sold from week 3 to week 6 by Cathy is <u>222.23 litres</u>.

Tips and Tricks for Addition Questions

When you've worked out an exact answer, you could check that your answer is sensible by using the rounding method to do a quick estimate.

Practice Questions

1) Katie buys a cycling helmet for £13.89, a bell for £3.35 and some gloves for £12.30.
   How much money does she spend?

   A £31.96   **B** £29.54   **C** £32.14   **D** £28.76   **E** £26.89

2) Rafid, Freia, Martin and John take part in a relay race.
   Rafid's leg took 12.37 seconds, Freia's leg took 11.88 seconds,
   Martin's leg took 13.24 seconds and John's leg took 10.94 seconds.
   What was their total time for the race?

Section One — Working with Numbers

Subtraction

Subtraction can get a bit tricky. All the more reason to get in lots of practice...

Warm-Up Activity

1) Choose <u>ten</u> numbers between <u>1 and 100</u>. Write them out on separate scraps of paper.
2) Lay the scraps of paper <u>face-down</u> on a table.
3) Turn over <u>two</u> scraps of paper and <u>subtract</u> the smaller number from the bigger number in your head. Use a calculator to <u>check</u> whether you got the answer right.
4) Turn the papers <u>back over</u> and <u>shuffle</u> them up a bit. Then pick <u>another two numbers</u>.
5) The game ends when you have <u>five correct answers</u>.

11+ Style Questions

> **Q** Emma has £13.10. She donates £2.21 to charity.
> How much money does Emma have left?
>
> | | | | | |
> |---|---|---|---|---|
> | A | £10.89 | | D | £11.79 |
> | B | £11.81 | | E | £10.79 |
> | C | £9.89 | | | |

Method 1

1) <u>Partition</u> the number that you are subtracting into its <u>units</u>, <u>tenths</u> and <u>hundredths</u>:

> £2.21 splits up into £2 + £0.20 + £0.01
>
> units   tenths   hundredths

2) <u>Subtract</u> each number <u>one at a time</u>:

> £13.10 − £2.00 = £11.10
> £11.10 − £0.20 = £10.90
> £10.90 − £0.01 = £10.89

Be careful here — you're changing the value in the units column as well as the tenths.

Your answer is £10.89 — option A.

Method 2

1) You can also subtract numbers by writing them in <u>columns</u>.
2) Write the <u>number you're subtracting from first</u> and make sure the decimal points <u>line up</u>.

> Subtract the numbers in each column starting from the right.
>
> $$1\overset{2}{\cancel{3}}\ .\ \overset{10}{\cancel{1}}\overset{10}{\cancel{0}}$$
> $$-\ \ \ 2\ .\ 2\ 1$$
> $$\overline{1\ 0\ .\ 8\ 9}$$
>
> If you have to subtract a bigger number from a smaller number, make an exchange from the next place value column.

Q Three people ran two 200 m races. Their times for race 1 are shown in the table.
All three ran faster in race 2.

Vanessa ran 1.8 seconds faster.
Rajpal ran 0.9 seconds faster.
Stacey ran 2.5 seconds faster.

Who had the fastest time in race 2?

Name	Race 1 (s)
Vanessa	25.3
Rajpal	24.2
Stacey	26.2

You could use a written method to work out the difference in time for each person, but it would take more time.

Method

1) For each person, you need to take the time they ran in <u>race 1</u>, and <u>subtract</u> the amount of time that they ran faster by.

2) You could use the <u>counting back method</u>. Start with each person's time for race 1 and <u>count back</u> in <u>easy steps</u> to get their time for race 2.

First subtract the whole number. Vanessa ran 1.8 seconds faster in race 2, so subtract 1 second.

Then remove the decimal part. After subtracting 1, Vanessa's time is 24.3 seconds and there are still 0.8 seconds to subtract. Take away 0.3 to get 24.0 seconds.

Vanessa:
$25.3 - 1 = 24.3$
$24.3 - 0.3 = 24.0$
$24.0 - 0.5 = 23.5$

Rajpal:
$24.2 - 0.2 = 24.0$
$24.0 - 0.7 = 23.3$

Stacey:
$26.2 - 2 = 24.2$
$24.2 - 0.2 = 24.0$
$24.0 - 0.3 = 23.7$

That leaves 0.5 still to subtract. Take this away to get her time for race 2.

3) <u>Rajpal</u> has the fastest time in race 2 (<u>23.3 seconds</u>).

You could also round the number you're subtracting to the nearest whole number, subtract it, then count on or back by the amount you rounded by. E.g. for Rajpal, $24.2 - 1 = 23.2$, then count on by 0.1 to get 23.3.

Tips and Tricks for Subtraction Questions

When there are options to choose from, it's sometimes quickest to use rounding to estimate the answer.

Practice Questions

1) Gavin's bath holds 75.63 litres of water when it is full. Gavin pours 48.28 litres of water into the bath. How many more litres of water would he need to fill the bath?
   A 27.45   B 27.75   C 26.95   D 28.15   E 27.35

2) The table shows the results of five students in two tests. Which student had the greatest increase in score between test 1 and test 2?

Name	Test 1 (%)	Test 2 (%)
Joe	57.6	61.5
Holly	66.2	65.8
Lucille	62.7	66.4
Dave	64.1	59.9
Anita	59.8	63.6

Multiplying and Dividing by 10, 100 and 1000

When you multiply or divide any number by 10, 100 or 1000, you just move the digits left or right.

Warm-Up Activity

Write down the following numbers in order from smallest to biggest.

6300

0.063

0.63

630

6.3

63

Move digits **Left** to **Multiply** by **10, 100** or **1000**

1) If you're multiplying a number by 10, move the digits <u>one place</u> to the <u>left</u>.

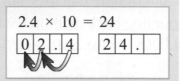

2) If you're multiplying a number by <u>100</u>, move the digits <u>two places</u> to the <u>left</u>.

Put a zero here to fill in the gap before the decimal point.

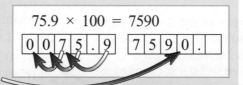

3) If you're multiplying a number by <u>1000</u>, move the digits <u>three places</u> to the <u>left</u>.

This time you need to put two zeros before the decimal point.

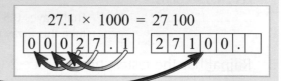

Move digits **Right** to **Divide** by **10, 100** or **1000**

1) If you're dividing a number by <u>10</u>, move the digits <u>one place</u> to the <u>right</u>.

Put a zero before the decimal point to fill in the gap.

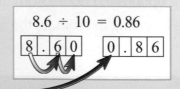

2) If you're dividing a number by <u>100</u>, move the digits <u>two places</u> to the <u>right</u>.

Put one zero before the decimal point and one zero after to fill in the gaps.

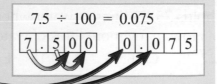

3) If you're dividing a number by <u>1000</u>, move the digits <u>three places</u> to the <u>right</u>.

Put a zero before the decimal point to fill in the gap.

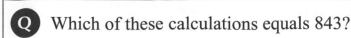

11+ Style *Questions*

> **Q** Which of these calculations equals 843?
>
> A $84300 \div 10$ D 0.0843×1000
> B 0.843×1000 E 0.843×100
> C $84300 \div 1000$

You might find it easier to think of this as moving the decimal place. E.g. Move the decimal place one place to the right to multiply by 10.

Method

1) Work out the answer to <u>each calculation</u>:

> A   Move each digit one place to the right: $84300 \div 10 = 8430$
> B   Move each digit three places to the left: $0.843 \times 1000 = 843$
> C   Move each digit three places to the right: $84300 \div 1000 = 84.3$
> D   Move each digit three places to the left: $0.0843 \times 1000 = 84.3$
> E   Move each digit two places to the left: $0.843 \times 100 = 84.3$

2) The correct answer is 0.843×1000 — option <u>B</u>.

> **Q** $301 \times 10 = \ldots\ldots\ldots \div 100$
> Which number should fill in the blank?

Method

1) Multiply <u>301 by 10</u> to work out the <u>first part</u> of the calculation.

> $301 \times 10 = 3010$ ← To multiply by ten, move each digit one place to the left.

2) The <u>second part</u> of the calculation must also <u>equal</u> 3010.

3) When you <u>divide</u> the missing number by <u>100</u>, it will equal <u>3010</u>.
   So, calculate the missing number by doing the <u>inverse operation</u> — multiplying by 100.

> $3010 \times 100 = 301\,000$ ← This time you are multiplying by 100, so each digit moves two places to the left.

4) That gives you the answer: <u>301 000</u>. You can check it's correct
   by dividing <u>301 000 by 100</u>. It should equal <u>3010</u>.

Practice Questions

1) Mark has sold 1000 tickets for a raffle. The tickets were sold in books of ten.
   In total, Mark collected £375 for all 1000 tickets. How much did one book cost?
   A £0.37   B £3.75   C £3.57   D £7.35   E £37.50

2) $4.2 \div 10 = \ldots\ldots\ldots \times 100$
   What number should fill in the blank?

Multiplication

There are a few ways that multiplication can be tested — these pages will show you the sorts of things that might come up, and how to tackle them.

Warm-Up Activity

1) Think of as many <u>different</u> multiplications as you can that will give the <u>numbers</u> on the cards.
2) See how many you can think of in <u>5 minutes</u>.

| 18 | 36 | 54 | 12 | 28 |

11+ Style Questions

> **Q** A DVD costs £3.99. How much will nine DVDs cost?
>
> A   £35.91   D   £35.97
> B   £36.00   E   £36.09
> C   £36.04

Quick Method

1) Round the cost of each DVD to the <u>nearest whole number</u>. Then multiply by <u>nine</u>.

> £3.99 rounds up to £4.00. £4.00 × 9 = £36.00

You added 1 penny for each DVD, and there were nine DVDs.

2) £36.00 is <u>not</u> the exact answer though. You added <u>nine pence</u> to this answer when you rounded the price of the DVDs. You need to <u>subtract nine pence</u> to reach the final answer.

> £36.00 − £0.09 = £35.91

Your answer is £35.91 — option A.

Written Method

1) You can multiply the numbers together in <u>columns</u>.
2) Make sure that you line up the <u>decimal point</u> and the <u>place value columns</u> in your answer.

Starting from the right, multiply the hundredths, tenths and units by 9.

$$\begin{array}{r} 3\,.\,7\,9 \\ \times \quad\quad 9 \\ \hline 3\,4\,.\,1\,1 \\ {\scriptstyle 7 \quad 8} \end{array}$$

9 × 9 = 81. If the answer is more than 9 the left hand digit is carried to the next column.

In the final column, the carried digit goes here. (9 × 3) + 7 = 34.

The carried digit gets added to the answer of the next column. Here, (9 × 7) + 8 = 71.

Q What is 12.4 × 6.3?

A	0.7812	D	781.2
B	7.812	E	7812
C	78.12		

Method

1) In each answer option, the <u>numbers</u> are the <u>same</u>, but the decimal point is in a <u>different place</u>.

2) This means you can <u>estimate</u> the answer by <u>rounding</u> the two numbers in the calculation to the <u>nearest whole number</u>, then <u>multiplying</u> them together.

> 12.4 is rounded down to 12.   6.3 is rounded down to 6. $12 \times 6 = 72$

3) The estimated answer is <u>72</u>. The only option that is <u>near</u> to 72 is <u>78.12</u> — option C. 78.12 must be the <u>exact answer</u>.

Q 526 × 24 = 12 624

This is a number fact.

What is 526 × 12?

Quick Method

1) Use the <u>number fact</u> to help you work out the answer to the question.

2) 12 is <u>half</u> of 24. So the answer to <u>526 × 12</u> will be <u>half</u> of the answer to <u>526 × 24</u>.

> $12\,624 \div 2 = 6312$ ⟹ $526 \times 12 = 6312$

Written Method

1) An alternative method would be to use <u>long multiplication</u>.

2) Line the numbers up in <u>columns</u> and put the <u>bigger number</u> on top.

3) Multiply <u>each digit</u> in the bigger number (starting from the right) with the <u>units</u> and <u>tens</u> of the smaller number:

Multiply each digit by 2.

Write the answer here.

```
      5 2 6
  ×     1 2
    1 0 5 2
        1
```

Then, multiply each number by 10.

Write the answer on the line below.

```
      5 2 6
  ×     1 2
    1 0 5 2
        1
    5 2 6 0
```

4) <u>Add</u> your two answers together to get the final answer.

```
      5 2 6
  ×     1 2
    1 0 5 2
        1
  + 5 2 6 0
    6 3 1 2
        1
```

You may have been taught a different method for written multiplication. That's fine — just use whichever one works best for you.

Q What is 47 × 30?

There's more about how to multiply by 10, 100 or 1000 on page 12.

Method 1

1) 30 is a <u>multiple of 10</u>. So multiply 47 by 10 to start off with.

$$47 \times 10 = 470$$

2) 30 is the <u>same</u> as 3 × 10, so <u>add together</u> 3 lots of 470.

$$470 + 470 + 470 = 1410$$

You could do this quickly in your head by rounding 470 up to 500, adding the numbers together, then subtracting 90.

Method 2

1) 30 is the <u>same</u> as 3 × 10, so first multiply 47 by <u>3</u>.

$$47 \times 3 = 141$$

You could do this quickly in your head by rounding 47 up to 50, doing the multiplication, then subtracting 9.

2) Then multiply the result by 10.

$$141 \times 10 = 1410$$

Tips and Tricks for Multiplication Questions

If a question gives you a number fact, it's a pretty big clue that there's a quick way to work out the answer. Look closely at how the numbers in the number fact are related to the numbers in the question.

Practice Questions

1) $3.5 \times 7.9 = 27.65$
   What is 350 × 79?

2) A toy robot costs £5.49. How much will six toy robots cost?
   A £32.94   **B** £30.30   **C** £33.00   **D** £31.94   **E** £32.96

3) What is 6.9 × 8.2?
   A 64.40   **B** 48.18   **C** 45.95   **D** 56.58   **E** 72.52

4) Each bookshelf in a library can hold 18 books.
   How many books can be held on 53 bookshelves?

Division

Division is the opposite of multiplication — you're splitting a number into groups.

Warm-Up Activity

1) Open up your money box (or find some counters). <u>Count</u> how many coins you have.
2) Start by <u>dividing</u> the coins into <u>groups of 5</u>. Count how many groups there are and make a note of the <u>remainder</u> if there is one.
3) Then do the same again with groups of <u>6</u>, <u>7</u> and <u>8</u>.

11+ Style Questions

> **Q** Each guinea pig cage holds 3 guinea pigs.
>
> How many cages would 124 guinea pigs need?

Quick Method

1) You need to <u>divide</u> 124 by 3, but 3 isn't a <u>factor</u> of 124.
2) <u>Partition</u> 124 into two numbers that are <u>easier</u> to work with. You need to find a number that's close to 124 and is a multiple of 3. You could split 124 into <u>120</u> and <u>4</u>.
3) Start by working out how many cages you'd need for <u>120 guinea pigs</u>.

> Using your 3 times table, you know that $12 \div 3 = 4$.
> 120 is 10 times bigger than 12, so $120 \div 3 = 40$.

4) Next, work out how many cages you'd need for the <u>remaining 4 guinea pigs</u>. Then <u>add</u> your two answers <u>together</u>.

> $4 \div 3 = 1$ remainder 1 $40 + 1$ remainder $1 = 41$ remainder 1

5) You still have a <u>remainder of 1</u> — so if you just have 41 cages there will be 1 poor guinea pig <u>without</u> a cage. You need <u>42 cages</u> so that every guinea pig has a cage.

Written Method

1) You can also use a written method to divide 124 by 3.

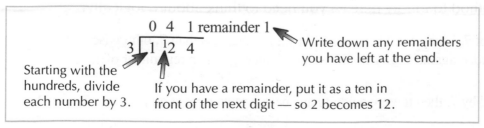

Starting with the hundreds, divide each number by 3.

If you have a remainder, put it as a ten in front of the next digit — so 2 becomes 12.

Write down any remainders you have left at the end.

2) 41 cages will leave one extra guinea pig without a cage, so the answer must be <u>42</u>.

Q Emily ran for a distance of 2123 metres. It took her 9 minutes.
To the nearest whole metre, how many metres did she run per minute?

Method

1) You need to <u>divide</u> the <u>total distance</u> Emily ran by the <u>length of time</u> it took her.

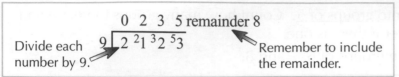

Divide each number by 9.

Remember to include the remainder.

2) The question asks for the answer to the <u>nearest whole metre</u>.
So, 235 remainder 8 should be <u>rounded up</u> to <u>236 metres</u>.

If the remainder is greater than half of the number you're dividing by, it should be rounded up. If it's less, it should be rounded down.

 Q What is 12.5 divided by 5?

Method

1) First, <u>convert</u> the decimal number into a <u>whole number</u> — this makes it <u>easier</u> to divide.

Multiply 12.5 by 10 to make a whole number. $12.5 \times 10 = 125$.

2) Then, find the <u>answer</u> to the <u>division</u>.

Find $125 \div 5$. Partition 125 into $100 + 25$ and divide each bit separately.
$100 \div 5 = 20$, $25 \div 5 = 5$. So $125 \div 5 = 20 + 5 = 25$.

3) Because you <u>multiplied 12.5 by 10</u> at the beginning, you've got to <u>divide</u> your answer <u>by 10</u>.

$25 \div 10 = 2.5$, so 12.5 divided by 5 = 2.5

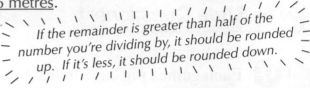

You could also use the written method here — just make sure you put the decimal point in the right place.

 Q Libby divides a number by a smaller number. Her answer has a remainder of 7.
Which of these numbers could Libby have divided by?

A 8   B 4   C 6   D 5   E 7

Method

There's <u>no clear method</u> to follow here — you need to think about it logically:

To get a remainder of 7, Libby can't have divided by a number less than 7, otherwise it could've been divided again. E.g. 4 would go into 7 once, giving a remainder of 3.

If Libby had divided by 7, then there wouldn't have been a remainder at all (because $7 \div 7 = 1$).

Libby must have divided by a number greater than 7. So the answer must be 8 — option A.

Q $3150 \div 9 = 350$

What is $9450 \div 9$?

This is similar to the method used to answer the number fact question on page 15.

Quick Method

1) Use the <u>number fact</u> to help you work out the answer to the question.

2) See if you can spot how the numbers in the two calculations are <u>related to each other</u>. 9450 is <u>three times larger</u> than 3150. So, the answer to $9450 \div 9$ will be <u>three times larger</u> than 350.

You could work this out by doing 300×3 and then 50×3. Then add the answers together. $\longrightarrow$ $350 \times 3 = 1050$ $\longrightarrow$ $9450 \div 9 = 1050$

Written Method

1) You could use a <u>written method</u> to divide 9450 by 9.

2) Write out the division and divide <u>each number</u> in 9450 by 9:

$$
\begin{array}{r}
1\ 0\ 5\ 0 \\
9\overline{)9\ 4^{4}5\ 0}
\end{array}
$$

The answer is 1050.

Divide each number by 9.

<u>Tips and Tricks for Division Questions</u>

It's not always obvious how you should work out the answer to division questions. Think carefully about what the question is asking you to do. Remember, sometimes you'll need to partition a larger number into smaller chunks that are easier to work with.

Practice Questions

1) What is $8.8 \div 4$?

2) A soft toy costs £1.30. How many soft toys can you buy with £14.50?

3) $19\,200 \div 16 = 1200$. What is $19\,200 \div 4$?
   A 600   **B** 2400   **C** 4800   **D** 7200   **E** 9600

4) Each level on a computer game takes 8 minutes to complete.
   If Jamil spent 264 minutes playing the computer game, how many levels does he complete?

Section One — Working with Numbers

Mixed Calculations

Mixed calculation questions will test all of your adding, subtracting, multiplying and dividing skills. But don't worry — there are some handy tricks you can learn to make them much easier.

Warm-Up Activity

1) Find a pack of <u>playing cards</u>.
2) Ask someone else to join you and take it in turns to pick <u>three cards</u>.
3) <u>Multiply together</u> the numbers on the <u>first two</u> cards you pick. Then <u>divide</u> the result by the number on the <u>third</u> card (Aces count as one and Jack, Queen and King all count as 10). Give yourself 1 point if you score <u>5 or more</u>.
4) The first player to get <u>5 points</u> is the winner.

BODMAS is Really Important

Operations are things like ×, ÷, + and −.

1) <u>BODMAS</u> tells you the <u>order</u> in which <u>operations</u> should be done in a <u>mixed calculation</u>.

> BODMAS = Brackets, Other, Division, Multiplication, Addition, Subtraction

'Other' is things like square numbers.

2) Work out anything in <u>Brackets</u> first, then <u>Other</u> things like square numbers, then <u>Divide</u> / <u>Multiply</u> groups of numbers before <u>Adding</u> or <u>Subtracting</u> them.

11+ Style Questions

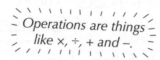

Q What is $7 + 12 \div (9 - 7) + 4^2$?

Take a look at page 22 if you're unsure about square numbers.

Method

You need to follow <u>BODMAS</u> to make sure you do the calculations in the <u>correct order</u>.

Do the bit in brackets first... $7 + 12 \div 2 + 4^2$ $9 - 7 = 2$

... then work out the square number... $7 + 12 \div 2 + 16$ $4^2 = 4 \times 4 = 16$

... next work out the division... $7 + 6 + 16$ $12 \div 2 = 6$

... then add all the remaining numbers together. $7 + 6 + 16 = 29$

Q What is $\dfrac{360}{40 \times 1.5}$?

Treat the top and bottom of a fraction as if they have brackets round them — so you do the calculations before you divide the top by the bottom.

Method

1) The calculation is displayed as a <u>fraction</u>, which means that you need to <u>divide</u> 360 by the product of 40×1.5.

2) First calculate 40×1.5. You could <u>partition</u> 1.5 into 1 and 0.5, then <u>add together</u> the products of the multiplications.

$40 \times 1 = 40$
$40 \times 0.5 = 20$ ← Multiplying by 0.5 is the same as halving a number.
$40 + 20 = 60$

3) Then divide 360 by 60.

$360 \div 60 = 6$ ← If you divide both 360 and 60 by 10, this is the same as $36 \div 6 = 6$.

Q $42 \times 603 + 58 \times 603 =$

A	1 206	C	34 974	E	60 300
B	25 326	D	54 270		

You could also use a written method or estimation to work out each of the steps of this calculation — but it would take a lot more time.

Method

Following the BODMAS rule you do each multiplication before adding.
But 42 and 58 are <u>both multiplied</u> by the same number, 603.
You can just add <u>42 and 58</u> and <u>multiply</u> this number by <u>603</u> to find the answer.

$42 + 58 = 100$. So $42 \times 603 + 58 \times 603$ simplifies to 100×603.
$100 \times 603 = 60\ 300$ — so the correct answer is option E.

<u>Tips and Tricks for Mixed Calculations</u>

Multiplying or dividing numbers by 10, 100 or 1000 can help to simplify a calculation. Remember though — when you get to the end of your calculation, you might need to do the opposite function to your answer to make it correct.

Practice Questions

1) What is $6 + 4 \times 3^2 \div (16 - 13)$?

2) $1450 \times 1.7 + 1450 \times 8.3 + 110 =$

Section One — Working with Numbers

Types of Number

It's really useful to know a few facts about different types of numbers.

Negative Numbers are Numbers Below 0

1) You can use <u>number lines</u> to compare the <u>values</u> of <u>negative numbers</u>.

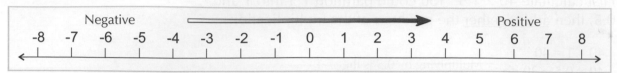

2) The numbers on the number line <u>increase</u> from <u>left to right</u>. So <u>-1</u> is <u>greater than -6</u>.

3) <u>Number lines</u> can be used to help you with calculations that involve <u>negative numbers</u>. For example to work out 2 − 9, just count back 9 places from 2 along the number line:

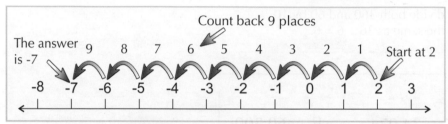

You can use **Symbols** to show whether one number is **Bigger** or **Smaller** than **Another**

There are <u>two symbols</u> you can use:

< means 'is less than'. For example, -3 is less than 2 or **-3 < 2**.
> means 'is greater than'. For example, 7 is greater than 5 or **7 > 5**.

Whole Numbers are either Odd or Even

Even numbers end in 0, 2, 4, 6 or 8. Odd numbers end in 1, 3, 5, 7 or 9.

1) An <u>even number</u> is any whole number that can be <u>exactly divided</u> by <u>two</u> to give another <u>whole number</u>. For example, <u>6</u> is an <u>even number</u> because 6 ÷ 2 = 3.

2) An <u>odd number</u> is any whole number that can't be <u>divided</u> by <u>two</u> to give another <u>whole number</u>. For example, <u>5</u> is an <u>odd number</u> because 5 ÷ 2 = 2.5.

A **Whole Number Multiplied** by **Itself** gives a **Square Number**

1) For example, if you <u>multiply 4 by itself</u> (4 × 4) you get <u>16</u> — a <u>square number</u>.

2) The <u>first 12 square numbers</u> are:

1	4	9	16	25	36	49	64	81	100	121	144
(1 × 1)	(2 × 2)	(3 × 3)	(4 × 4)	(5 × 5)	(6 × 6)	(7 × 7)	(8 × 8)	(9 × 9)	(10 × 10)	(11 × 11)	(12 × 12)

3) You can show a number is squared using a <u>small 2</u>, e.g. <u>five squared</u> (5 × 5) can be written as "5^2".

11+ *Style* Questions

> **Q** The sum of the first three square numbers is 14.
> What is the sum of the first 6 square numbers?

--- **Method** ---

1) You're told that the first three square numbers add up to 14. You need to work out the sum of the 4th, 5th and 6th square numbers and add it to 14. The 4th, 5th and 6th square numbers are:

4^2 $4 \times 4 = 16$
5^2 $5 \times 5 = 25$
6^2 $6 \times 6 = 36$

2) Now add 14 to the sum of the 4th, 5th and 6th square numbers:

$16 + 25 + 36 = 77$
$14 + 77 = 91$

> **Q** Which of these numbers will go into
> the shaded section of the Venn diagram?
>
> A 4   D 13
> B 7   E 27
> C 9

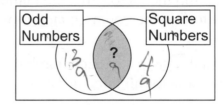

--- **Method** ---

1) Data that's put into a Venn diagram must match its labels.
Odd numbers must go in the left-hand circle of this Venn diagram, and square numbers can only go in the right-hand circle. Where the circles overlap the data must match both labels — so numbers in this section must be odd and square. Data that doesn't match any of the labels must go in the box outside the circles.

2) Numbers that are both odd and square must go in the shaded section. Start off by working out which of the options are square numbers.

4 and 9 are both square numbers: $4 = 2 \times 2$, $9 = 3 \times 3$.

3) Then, work out which of 4 and 9 is an odd number.

4 is even because it's divisible by 2. 9 is odd because it isn't divisible by 2 — C is the answer.

Practice Question

1) The table shows which floor of a tall building different people work on.

How many floors higher is the person who works on the highest floor, than the person who works on the lowest floor?

Person	Floor
Sheila	13
Heather	15
Peter	-1
Julia	5
Archie	-4

Factors, Multiples and Primes

Factors, multiples and primes are more types of number you need to know about.

Factors of a number are Whole Numbers that divide Exactly into it

1) The factors of a number are all the whole numbers that divide into that number exactly (so there's no remainder). For example the factors of 9 are 1, 3 and 9:

$$9 \div 1 = 9$$
$$9 \div 3 = 3$$
$$9 \div 9 = 1$$

2) If a question asks for the common factors of some numbers, you need to find the factors that the numbers all share. Here's how to find the common factors of 12, 24 and 36:

> Find the factors of each number, then work out which factors are the same for all three numbers.
>
> > The factors of 12 are: 1, 2, 3, 4, 6 and 12.
> > The factors of 24 are: 1, 2, 3, 4, 6, 8, 12 and 24.
> > The factors of 36 are: 1, 2, 3, 4, 6, 9, 12, 18 and 36.
> > 1, 2, 3, 4, 6 and 12 are all common factors of 12, 24 and 36.

Remember to include the number itself in the list of factors.

3) The highest common factor (HCF) is just the biggest number that will divide into all the numbers in the question. In the example above, the HCF of 12, 24 and 36 is 12.

A Multiple is the Result of Multiplying one Whole Number by another

1) The multiples of a number are just the times table for that number, e.g. multiples of 4 are 4, 8, 12, 16 etc.

2) If a question asks for some common multiples of some numbers, you need to find multiples that the numbers all share. Here's how to find some common multiples of 4 and 6:

> Find the first few multiples of each number and check if any of them are the same. If not, work out a few more multiples, then try again.
>
> > The first six multiples of 4 are: 4, 8, 12, 16, 20 and 24.
> > The first five multiples of 6 are: 6, 12, 18, 24, 30.
> > So the first two common multiples of 4 and 6 are 12 and 24.

3) The lowest common multiple (LCM) is just the smallest multiple that the numbers in the question share. In the example above, the LCM of 4 and 6 is 12.

Prime Numbers *only have* Two Factors

1) A prime number is a number with exactly two factors — the number itself and one. For example, 23 is a prime number — the only factors of 23 are 1 and 23.

2) 1 is NOT a prime number — it doesn't have exactly two factors.

3) Apart from 2 and 5, all prime numbers end in 1, 3, 7 or 9 (but not all numbers ending in 1, 3, 7 or 9 are prime numbers).

4) The only even prime number is 2.

> The first ten prime numbers are: 2, 3, 5, 7, 11, 13, 17, 19, 23 and 29.

5) Whole numbers that aren't prime are made up of prime numbers multiplied together — these prime numbers are called prime factors. Here's how to find the prime factors of 40:

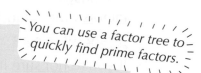
You can use a factor tree to quickly find prime factors.

Write down any factor pair of 40, then keep splitting the factors until they are all prime numbers.

$40 = 5 \times 8$
5 is a prime number. It is a prime factor of 40.
8 isn't a prime number, so split this into a factor pair:
$40 = 5 \times 2 \times 4$
2 is a prime number. It is a prime factor of 40.
4 isn't a prime number, so split this into a factor pair:
$40 = 5 \times 2 \times 2 \times 2$

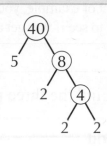

11+ Style Questions

Q Two of the numbers are missing from this sorting diagram.

	Multiple of 3	Not a Multiple of 3
Factor of 66	3 6 **?** C	2 11 22
Not Factor of 66	**?** A	7

Which of the following could be the missing numbers?

A 36 and 12 ×   D 33 and 12
B 3 and 25 ×   E 81 and 19
C 66 and 33

Method

1) Both of the missing numbers are multiples of 3, one is a factor of 66 and one isn't. Start off by finding which of the answer options have two multiples of 3.

    3, 12, 33, 36, 66 and 81 are all multiples of 3. 19 and 25 are not.
    Options A, C and D all have two multiples of 3.

2) Now work out which one of these options has only one factor of 66.

    A   36 and 12 are not factors of 66.
    C   66 and 33 are both factors of 66.
    D   33 is a factor of 66, but 12 is not — D is the answer.

Section Two — Number Knowledge

Q Emily bought some sweets and gave them all away to her friends. Each friend got an equal number of sweets and they were all given more than one sweet. How many sweets could she have bought?

19   23   24   29   31

The question doesn't say how many friends Emily has — but she has more than one because it says she has "friends" and not "a friend".

Method

1) You might recognise that <u>all</u> of the amounts, <u>except 24</u>, are <u>prime numbers</u> (prime numbers have no factors other than one and the number itself).

   If the number of sweets is a prime number, e.g. 23, then they can only be equally distributed between one friend or a group of 23 friends. The question shows that there is more than one friend and they all get more than one sweet. So none of these are right.

2) The <u>answer</u> to the question is <u>24</u> because that is the <u>only number</u> that has any <u>factors</u> other than <u>1</u> and <u>itself</u>. For example, if Emily had 24 sweets she could give <u>8</u> friends <u>3</u> sweets each, or <u>4</u> friends could have <u>6</u> sweets each, etc.

3) If you're <u>not sure</u> if a number is <u>prime</u> then you can try to find the number's <u>factors</u>.

   For example, you could work out if 19 has any factors other than 1 or 19. Divide 19 by possible factors to see if you get a whole number. This will take time so it'd be useful to memorise some prime numbers.

Q Find the three prime numbers that multiply together to give 52.

Method

1) You need to find the set of <u>prime numbers</u> that <u>multiplies together</u> to make 52.

2) First find any <u>factor pair</u> of 52.

   | $52 = 2 \times 26$ | 2 is a prime number, but 26 isn't.

3) <u>Split</u> any factors that aren't prime into more factor pairs until you're <u>only left with prime numbers</u>.

   | $52 = 2 \times 2 \times 13$ | 26 splits to 2 × 13, which are both prime numbers.

4) You've now got three primes that multiply to give 52, so you can stop. $2 \times 2 \times 13$ is called the <u>prime factorisation</u> of 52.

Practice Questions

1) Which of these statements is true?

   A All factors of 24 are multiples of 2.
   B 13 and 52 have no common factors.
   C All numbers ending in a 3 are multiples of 3.
   D The highest common factor of 36 and 18 is 9.
   E A prime number can be a multiple of 3.

2) Which of these numbers is not a factor of 72?

   A 4   **B** 6   **C** 7   **D** 8   **E** 9

Section Two — Number Knowledge

Fractions

Fractions are a bit tricky, but you'll be fine once you've learnt the basics.

Fractions are Parts of a Whole Number

1) A <u>fraction</u> looks like this:

The <u>bottom number</u> of a fraction is the <u>denominator</u>. It tells you how many equal parts something is split into.  The <u>top number</u> of a fraction is the <u>numerator</u>. It tells you how many equal parts you've got.

2) Fractions can be shown using <u>shapes</u>.

This triangle is split into 9 equal parts. 4 out of the 9 parts are shaded. So the fraction of the triangle that's shaded is ⁴⁄₉.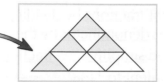

3) To find a <u>fraction</u> of a <u>number</u> (e.g. four-fifths of 15), <u>divide</u> the <u>number</u> by the <u>fraction's denominator</u>. Then <u>multiply</u> the result by the <u>fraction's numerator</u>.

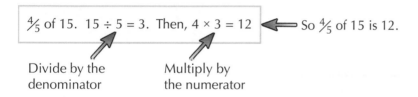

⁴⁄₅ of 15. 15 ÷ 5 = 3. Then, 4 × 3 = 12 ⬅ So ⁴⁄₅ of 15 is 12.

Divide by the denominator

Multiply by the numerator

Alternatively, you can multiply by the numerator then divide by the denominator.

4) You can see this more clearly with a <u>diagram</u>:

To find ⁴⁄₅ of 15 apples, start by dividing 15 by 5. That gives you 5 groups of 3 apples. So ⁴⁄₅ = 4 groups of 3 apples, or 12 apples.

Some Fractions are Bigger Than 1

1) You can write <u>fractions</u> that are <u>bigger than 1</u> as <u>improper fractions</u> or <u>mixed numbers</u>.

2) <u>Improper fractions</u> have a numerator that's <u>bigger</u> than the denominator. For example:

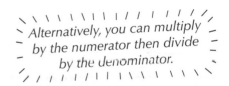 ¹³⁄₈

1 whole is the same as 8 eighths (or ⁸⁄₈) so this fraction is greater than 1. 13 eighths is the same as one whole plus another ⁵⁄₈.

3) <u>Mixed numbers</u> have <u>both</u> a whole number and a fraction. For example:

 1 ⁵⁄₈

This fraction is greater than 1 — there is 1 whole plus another ⁵⁄₈.

Equivalent Fractions are *Fractions* which are *Equal*

1) For example, $\frac{1}{4}$ and $\frac{2}{8}$ are <u>equivalent fractions</u> because they're <u>equal</u>. You can show this using <u>shapes</u>:

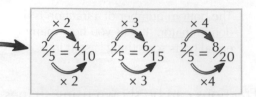

2) To find an <u>equivalent fraction</u>, <u>multiply</u> the <u>numerator</u> and the <u>denominator</u> by the <u>same number</u>. So $\frac{2}{5}$ is <u>equivalent</u> to $\frac{4}{10}$, $\frac{6}{15}$ and $\frac{8}{20}$.

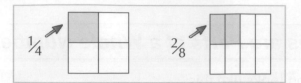

$$\overset{\times 2}{\frac{2}{5}=\frac{4}{10}}_{\times 2} \qquad \overset{\times 3}{\frac{2}{5}=\frac{6}{15}}_{\times 3} \qquad \overset{\times 4}{\frac{2}{5}=\frac{8}{20}}_{\times 4}$$

3) You can also find <u>equivalent fractions</u> by <u>dividing</u> both the <u>numerator</u> and the <u>denominator</u> by the <u>same number</u>. This is called <u>simplifying</u> a <u>fraction</u>. For example $\frac{55}{100}$ is equivalent to $\frac{11}{20}$.

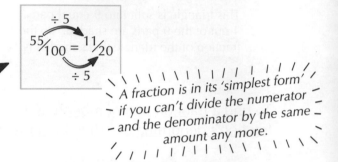

$$\overset{\div 5}{\frac{55}{100}=\frac{11}{20}}_{\div 5}$$

A fraction is in its 'simplest form' if you can't divide the numerator and the denominator by the same amount any more.

You can **Add** *and* **Subtract Fractions**

1) <u>Adding</u> and <u>subtracting</u> fractions is easy if they <u>both</u> have the <u>same denominator</u>. All you need to do is <u>add</u> or <u>subtract</u> the <u>numerators</u> and keep the <u>denominator</u> the <u>same</u>.

$$\frac{2}{5}+\frac{2}{5}=\frac{4}{5} \qquad\qquad \frac{4}{5}-\frac{1}{5}=\frac{3}{5}$$

2) To <u>add</u> or <u>subtract</u> fractions which have <u>different denominators</u>, change them so they have the <u>same denominator</u>. You can do this by making them into <u>equivalent fractions</u>.

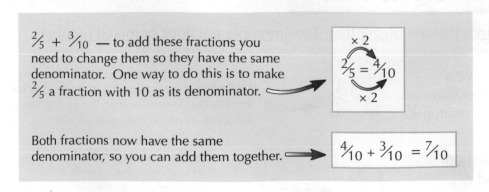

$\frac{2}{5}+\frac{3}{10}$ — to add these fractions you need to change them so they have the same denominator. One way to do this is to make $\frac{2}{5}$ a fraction with 10 as its denominator.

$$\overset{\times 2}{\frac{2}{5}=\frac{4}{10}}_{\times 2}$$

Both fractions now have the same denominator, so you can add them together. $\longrightarrow$ $\frac{4}{10}+\frac{3}{10}=\frac{7}{10}$

11+ Style Questions

 Q Jenny has made 108 cupcakes. She sells 72 of them at the school fair.
What fraction of her cupcakes did she sell?
Give your answer as a fraction in its simplest form.

Method

1) Jenny sold <u>72 out of 108</u> or $^{72}/_{108}$ cupcakes.

2) <u>Simplify</u> the fraction by finding <u>common factors</u>.

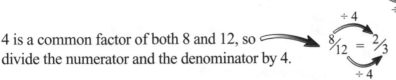

9 is a common factor of both 72 and 108, so
divide the numerator and the denominator by 9.

$$^{72}/_{108} = {}^{8}/_{12}$$

4 is a common factor of both 8 and 12, so
divide the numerator and the denominator by 4.

$$^{8}/_{12} = {}^{2}/_{3}$$

3) 2 and 3 don't have any common factors — the fraction is in its <u>simplest form</u>.

 Q A coat is originally priced at £32.
Its price is reduced to ¾ of the original price.
What is the price of the coat now?

Method

1) You need to find ¾ of <u>£32</u>. First, <u>divide 32</u> by the <u>denominator</u> of the <u>fraction</u>.

4 is the denominator in ¾ . So, 32 ÷ 4 = 8.
This means that ¼ of £32 = £8.

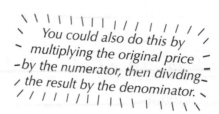
You could also do this by multiplying the original price by the numerator, then dividing the result by the denominator.

2) Now <u>multiply 8</u> by the <u>numerator</u>.

If ¼ = 8, then ¾ is 3 × 8 = 24.

3) The coat costs <u>£24</u>.

Practice Questions

1) Lydia and Rose each have a pie. Their pies are exactly the same size.
Lydia gave two-fifths of her pie to Gemma. Rose gave Gemma one-fifth of her pie.
Which statement is correct?

A Gemma has more pie than Lydia.   D Gemma has the same amount of pie as Rose.
B Gemma has more pie than Rose.   E Gemma has the same amount of pie as Lydia.
C Lydia has more pie than Rose.   F Lydia has the same amount of pie as Rose.

2) Ilya and Alex have two bags of apples. Each bag contains 6 apples.
Ilya takes ¼ of the apples. Alex takes ⅔ of the apples.
How many apples are left?

A 0   B 1   C 2   D 3   E 4

Section Two — Number Knowledge

Ratio and Proportion

The difference between ratio and proportion can be tricky, so read this page carefully.

Ratios Compare One Part to Another Part

1) Ratios look like this:

You read this as '1 to 3'. It means there's one of the first type of thing for every three of the second type.

$$1:3$$

2) They are most clearly shown using shapes or objects:

The diagram shows that for every two limes there are six lemons.

So for every lime there are three lemons.
The ratio is 1 lime to 3 lemons — which you write as 1:3.

3) Finding equivalent ratios is a lot like finding equivalent fractions (see page 28). You have to multiply or divide all the parts of the ratio by the same number.

If there were 12 lemons, how many limes would there be?

$\times 4$ 3 lemons for every 1 lime $\times 4$

12 lemons for every ? limes

Like with fractions, both parts of the ratio have been multiplied by the same number — so there would be $1 \times 4 = 4$ limes.

Proportions Compare a Part to the Whole Thing

1) Proportions are written like this:

The 4 represents the whole thing and the 1 represents a part of the whole thing.

$$1 \text{ in every } 4$$

2) In the example above, 2 in every 8 fruits are limes, which is the same as 1 in every 4.

3) Proportions are another way of writing fractions. The proportion '1 in every 4' is the same as the fraction $\frac{1}{4}$. So you can answer proportion questions as you would fractions questions.

If there were 24 fruits, how many limes would there be?

The proportion of fruits that are limes is 1 in every 4, or $\frac{1}{4}$.

To find $\frac{1}{4}$ of 24, divide 24 by the denominator. ⟶ $24 \div 4 = 6$.

You don't need to multiply by the numerator here, because it's 1.

There would be 6 limes if there were 24 fruits.

11+ Style Questions

> **Q** Divide £490 in the ratio 4 : 3.

Method

1) First <u>add together</u> the numbers in the ratio to find out <u>how many parts</u> £490 needs to be divided into.

$$4 + 3 = 7$$

2) Next divide the total amount by 7 to find out how much <u>one part is</u>.

$$£490 \div 7 = £70$$

3) Then multiply £70 by <u>4</u> to find out how much <u>four parts</u> are, and by <u>3</u> to find out how much <u>three parts</u> are.

$$£70 \times 4 = £280$$
$$£70 \times 3 = £210$$

4) The answer is <u>£280 : £210</u>.

> **Q** 8 copies of the same magazine cost £16.40. How much will 3 copies cost?

Method

1) Divide the <u>total cost</u> by 8 to work out how much <u>one magazine costs</u>.

$$£16.40 \div 8 = £2.05$$

2) Then multiply by three to find the <u>cost</u> of <u>3 magazines</u>.

$$£2.05 \times 3 = £6.15$$

You could partition the costs to make them easier and quicker to multiply and divide.

48 : 96
6 : 12   ℓ : 2

Practice Questions

1) A farmer has 48 orange Highland cows and 96 black and white cows. What is the ratio of orange cows to black and white cows? Write your answer in its simplest form.

2) Maya has a box of coloured building blocks. 5 in every 7 of them are green. If there are 84 blocks in total, how many green blocks are there?

Percentages, Fractions and Decimals

You can write a proportion of something as a decimal, a fraction or a percentage. This page will show you how percentages, fractions and decimals are related, and how to convert between them.

You can **Convert** between **Percentages**, **Fractions** and **Decimals**

Decimals can be Converted into Percentages

1) To turn a <u>decimal</u> into a <u>percentage</u>, <u>multiply</u> the <u>decimal</u> by <u>100</u>, e.g. $0.53 \times 100 = \underline{53\%}$.

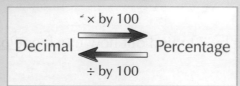

2) <u>Divide</u> the <u>percentage</u> by <u>100</u> to get back to the <u>decimal</u>, e.g. $72\% = 72 \div 100 = \underline{0.72}$.

Fractions can be Converted into Percentages

1) Converting fractions with <u>100</u> as the <u>denominator</u> into <u>percentages</u> is <u>easy</u>. The <u>numerator</u> is the <u>percentage</u>, e.g. $^{23}\!/_{100} = \underline{23\%}$.

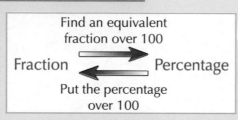

"Per cent" just means "out of 100" — it's usually written as %. So 17 per cent is 17 out of 100, which can also be written as 17%.

2) For other fractions, just make an <u>equivalent fraction</u> (see p.28) with <u>100</u> as the <u>denominator</u>.

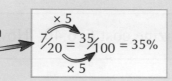

$$\overset{\times 5}{^{7}\!/_{20}} = ^{35}\!/_{100} = 35\%$$
$$\times 5$$

3) You can write <u>any</u> <u>percentage</u> as a <u>fraction</u>. Put the <u>percentage</u> on the <u>top</u> (the <u>numerator</u>) and <u>100</u> on the <u>bottom</u> (the <u>denominator</u>), e.g. $\underline{17\%} = ^{17}\!/_{100}$.

Fractions can also be Converted into Decimals

1) To <u>convert</u> a <u>fraction</u> into a <u>decimal</u>, you can often just find an <u>equivalent fraction</u> with <u>100</u> as its <u>denominator</u>.

Find the equivalent fraction over 100 and divide its numerator by 100

Fraction ⟶ Decimal

× by 100 and put this number over 100

2) Then <u>divide</u> the <u>numerator</u> by <u>100</u> to get the <u>decimal</u>.

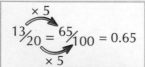

$$\overset{\times 5}{^{13}\!/_{20}} = ^{65}\!/_{100} = 0.65$$
$$\times 5$$

3) Sometimes you won't be able to find an <u>equivalent fraction</u> with 100 as its denominator, e.g. $^{5}\!/_{8}$. In this case you will need to <u>divide</u> the <u>numerator</u> by the <u>denominator</u>.

$$^{5}\!/_{8} = 8\overline{)5.0^{2}0^{4}0} = 0.625$$

4) To convert a <u>decimal</u> into a <u>fraction</u> you just <u>multiply</u> the decimal by <u>100</u>, then put this as the <u>numerator</u> above a <u>denominator of 100</u>. E.g. $\underline{0.29} = ^{29}\!/_{100}$.

(If the decimal has <u>more than 2</u> decimal places, multiply by a <u>bigger number</u> and put that as the denominator — e.g. $0.625 \times \underline{1000} = 625$, so $0.625 = ^{625}\!/_{1000}$)

These are very common fractions as percentages and decimals — make sure you know them:

$\frac{1}{4} = 25\%$ or 0.25 $\quad$ $\frac{3}{4} = 75\%$ or 0.75 $\quad$ $\frac{1}{2} = 50\%$ or 0.5 $\quad$ $\frac{1}{10} = 10\%$ or 0.1 $\quad$ $\frac{1}{5} = 20\%$ or 0.2

11+ Style Questions

Q What is $4\frac{4}{5}$ as a decimal?

Method

1) Change the <u>fraction</u> part to a <u>decimal</u>.

   Find an <u>equivalent fraction</u> with <u>100</u> as the denominator.

   Next <u>divide</u> the numerator of the equivalent fraction <u>by 100</u>.

   $$80 \div 100 = 0.8$$

2) <u>Add the whole number</u> part.

   $$4\frac{4}{5} = 4 + 0.8 = 4.8$$

Q Which one of these is the greatest?

   A $\frac{1}{5}$ of 45   B 25% of 40   C $\frac{1}{3}$ of 30   D 80% of 20   E $\frac{3}{4}$ of 20

Method

1) Work out the value of <u>each option</u> which involves a <u>fraction</u>. To work out the <u>fraction</u> of a <u>number</u> you need to <u>divide</u> the <u>number</u> by the <u>denominator</u> and <u>multiply</u> it by the <u>numerator</u>.

A: $\frac{1}{5}$ of 45	$45 \div 5 = 9$	$9 \times 1 = 9$
C: $\frac{1}{3}$ of 30	$30 \div 3 = 10$	$10 \times 1 = 10$
E: $\frac{3}{4}$ of 20	$20 \div 4 = 5$	$5 \times 3 = 15$

2) Work out the value of <u>each option</u> which involves a <u>percentage</u>. To work out the <u>percentage</u> of a number you could <u>convert</u> the <u>percentage</u> to a <u>fraction</u>. Then follow the method for working out the <u>fraction</u> of a number.

B: 25% of 40 is the same as $\frac{1}{4}$ of 40	$40 \div 4 = 10$	$10 \times 1 = 10$
D: 80% of 20 is the same as $\frac{8}{10}$ of 20	$20 \div 10 = 2$	$2 \times 8 = 16$

   Alternatively, you could find 10% and 5% and use those values to make the percentage you need.
   E.g. 25% = 10% + 10% + 5%

3) The answer is <u>D</u> because <u>80%</u> of <u>20</u> is the <u>greatest number</u>.

Q A bottle of tomato sauce contains 12% sugar.
What fraction of the tomato sauce is sugar?

A $^{12}/_{50}$ B $^{6}/_{50}$ C $^{24}/_{100}$ D $^{24}/_{50}$ E $^{3}/_{50}$

Method

1) First <u>convert</u> the percentage into a fraction.

> Convert 12% into a fraction. $12\% = \,^{12}/_{100}$.

2) Look at the options — <u>none</u> of them are $^{12}/_{100}$, which
   means that one of them must be <u>equivalent</u> to it.

3) The answer <u>can't</u> be <u>option C</u> — $^{12}/_{100}$ is less than $^{24}/_{100}$.

4) All the other options have a denominator of <u>50</u>,
   so <u>simplify</u> $^{12}/_{100}$ so it has a denominator of 50.

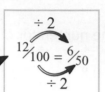

$$^{12}/_{100} = \,^{6}/_{50}$$

5) The answer is option <u>B</u>

Tips and Tricks for Percentages, Fractions and Decimals

Memorising some fractions as decimals and percentages
will help you answer some questions much faster.

Practice Questions

1) What percentage of this triangle is shaded?

   A 10%   **B** 20%   **C** 25%   **D** 30%   **E** 40%

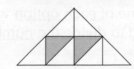

2) Marek asked all the children in Year 5
   what their favourite colour was.
   He made a chart to show his results.

   There are 90 children in Year 5.

   How many children chose pink
   as their favourite colour?

   A 12   **B** 18   **C** 27   **D** 30   **E** 33

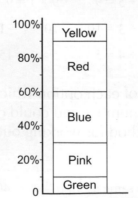

3) Which one of these is the smallest?

   A 25% of 4   **B** ¾ of 8   **C** ⅖ of 10   **D** 10% of 25   **E** ⅔ of 18

Algebra

Algebra isn't as scary as it sounds. Learn how it works and then practise, practise, practise...

Warm-Up Activity

Fill in the boxes so that the calculations are correct.

$\boxed{7} \times 6 = 48$

$\boxed{72} - 19 = 43$

$\boxed{8} \times 5 = 40$

$84 \div \boxed{12} = 7$

$46 + \boxed{27} = 73$

$34 - 16 = \boxed{18}$

Algebra is using **Letters** or **Symbols** to **Represent Numbers**

1) Algebra uses <u>letters</u> or <u>symbols</u> to <u>represent</u> numbers that you don't know.

2) An <u>algebraic expression</u> contains both <u>numbers</u> and <u>letters</u> or <u>symbols</u>. For example, if z is an unknown number you want to add 3 to, an <u>expression</u> could be:

$\boxed{z + 3}$

Sometimes there might just be an empty box to fill in to represent a missing number.

3) Algebra <u>doesn't</u> always use <u>multiplication signs</u> before letters or symbols. You just write the number <u>next to</u> the letter or symbol. For example:

$3\triangle$ means $3 \times \triangle$

$2ab$ means $2 \times a \times b$

$\frac{1}{2}x$ means $\frac{1}{2} \times x$

4) A <u>letter</u> or symbol written <u>over</u> a <u>number</u> means that you have to <u>divide</u> by that number. For example:

$\frac{x}{8}$ means $x \div 8$

5) Algebraic expressions also use <u>square numbers</u>. These show that a letter or symbol is <u>multiplied by itself</u>.

$\bullet^2$ means $\bullet \times \bullet$

6) <u>Brackets</u> are used to keep parts of an expression <u>together</u>. You should always work out the part in brackets <u>first</u>. For example:

$3(a + b)$ means $(a + b) + (a + b) + (a + b)$

Work out the part in brackets first $(a + b)$, and then find 3 lots of the answer.

7) You can <u>write expressions</u> to show what's happening in a word problem. For example:

I think of a number, add 2, divide by 3 then subtract 10. Write an expression to show this word problem.

Use a letter to represent the missing number, e.g. z.

Build up the expression bit-by-bit.

$z + 2$ — First, 2 is added to the number.

Then the result is divided by 3. — $\dfrac{z + 2}{3}$

$\dfrac{z + 2}{3} - 10$ — Then 10 is subtracted.

Do the **Opposite Operation** to solve an **Equation**

1) Equations have an <u>equals sign</u> in them to show that the values on the <u>left</u> hand side are <u>equal</u> to the values on the <u>right</u> hand side.

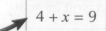
$4 + x = 9$

x represents a number that you don't know. When you add 4 to *x* you get 9.

2) You can <u>solve algebraic equations</u> by finding the <u>value</u> of the letter.

3) You need to remove parts of the equation until the <u>letter</u> is left <u>on its own</u> on one side of the equals sign.

4) To remove part of an equation, do the <u>opposite operation</u> to <u>both sides</u> of the equation. For example:

+ and – are opposites, and × and ÷ are opposites.

$$a + 4 = 20$$
$$a + 4 - 4 = 20 - 4$$
$$a = 16$$

The opposite of + 4 is – 4, so subtract 4 from both sides.

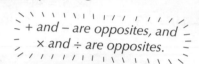
$$\bigstar - 4 = 20$$
$$\bigstar - 4 + 4 = 20 + 4$$
$$\bigstar = 24$$

The opposite of – 4 is + 4, so add 4 to both sides.

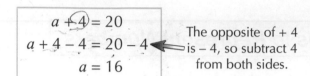
$$4 \times \ = 20$$
$$4 \bigcirc \div 4 = 20 \div 4$$
$$\bigcirc = 5$$

The opposite of × 4 is ÷ 4, so divide both sides by 4.

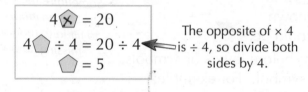
$$x \div 4 = 20$$
$$x \div 4 \times 4 = 20 \times 4$$
$$x = 80$$

The opposite of ÷ 4 is × 4, so multiply both sides by 4.

A **Formula** is Used to Work Out an **Amount**

1) A <u>formula</u> tells you how to work out <u>one quantity</u> when you know a <u>different quantity</u>. For example, the formula below is for working out how many wheels a group of cars has altogether.

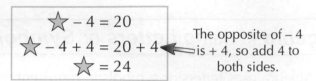
w = total number of wheels $w = 4c$ *c* = number of cars

2) You can <u>substitute</u> different known values into a formula to <u>work out</u> the unknown value. For example:

How many wheels do 8 cars have?
$w = 4c$ There are 8 cars, so *c* = 8.
$= 4 \times 8$ Substitute 8 for *c* in the formula.
$w = 32$ wheels altogether

How many wheels do 4 cars have?
$w = 4c$ There are 4 cars, so *c* = 4.
$= 4 \times 4$ Substitute 4 for *c* in the formula.
$w = 16$ wheels altogether

3) You can <u>write formulas</u> to help you <u>solve</u> word problems. For example:

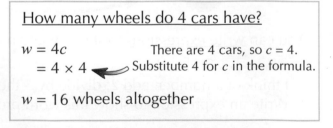

Spiders have 8 legs.
Write a formula for the total number of legs, *l*, of *t* spiders.

Total number of legs = number of spiders × 8   This is the formula in words.

$l = t \times 8$ ...or... $l = 8t$ Substitute the letters in to create the formula.

11+ Style Questions

Q At a restaurant, a hamburger costs £3 and a hot dog costs £2. Which expression gives the total cost, in pounds, of buying x hamburgers and y hot dogs?

A $2x + y$ B $5y - x$ C $3xy$ D $3x + 2y$ E $x \times y$

Method

1) Start by finding the cost (in pounds) of <u>x hamburgers</u>:

Cost of hamburgers = $3x$ The cost of the hamburgers is the number you're buying (x) multiplied by the price (£3). So this should be written as $3x$.

2) Next, add the cost (in pounds) of <u>y hot dogs</u>.

$3x + 2y$ Each hot dog costs £2, so the price of y hot dogs is $2y$ pounds.

3) That gives you the <u>finished expression</u>. The correct answer is <u>$3x + 2y$</u> — option <u>D</u>.

Q Solve the equation below to find the value of z.

$4 + 2z = 16$

Quick Method

The quickest way is just to use your <u>knowledge of maths</u> to <u>reason out</u> the answer.

1) $4 + 2z = 16$ Think "<u>what do you add to 4 to make 16?</u>" — it's 12, so $2z$ is the same as 12.

2) $2z = 12$ Think "<u>2 times what is 12?</u>" — it's 6, so z is the same as 6.

$z = 6$

Written Method

1) You need to <u>remove</u> parts of the equation so that the letter is left <u>on its own</u>.

$4 + 2z = 16$

2) The opposite of + 4 is – 4, so <u>subtract 4</u> from both sides

$4 + 2z - 4 = 16 - 4$ → $2z = 12$

3) The opposite of × 2 is ÷ 2, so <u>divide</u> both sides <u>by 2</u>.

$2z \div 2 = 12 \div 2$ → $z = 6$

Q A farm calculates the cost of eggs in pence (C) using this formula:

$C = 40 + 2x^2$

x is the number of eggs bought.

A man buys ⑨ eggs. What is the total cost in pounds?

Method

1) The man buys <u>9 eggs</u>, so <u>change x</u> in the formula to <u>9</u>.

$C = 40 + 2 \times 9^2$

2) Work out the calculation <u>one part at a time</u>. Remember to follow BODMAS (see page 20).

First, work out 9^2...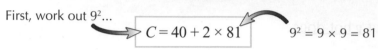

$C = 40 + 2 \times 81$ $9^2 = 9 \times 9 = 81$

... then do the multiplication...

$C = 40 + 162$ $2 \times 81 = 162$

... then work out the addition to find the cost in pence...

$C = 202$ $162 + 40 = 202$

... then divide by 100 to find the cost in pounds.

$C = 202p = £2.02$

Don't forget this last step. The question asked for the answer in pounds.

Tips and Tricks for Algebra Questions

When you have to solve an equation, you can check that your answer is correct by substituting it back into the original equation.

Practice Questions

1) The cost (in pounds) of calling out an electrician (C) is given by the formula: $C = 25 + 10h + p$ where h is the number of hours and p is the cost (in pounds) of any parts.
   What is the cost of the electrician when they work for 3 hours and need £20 worth of parts?

2) Solve the following equation to find the value of x.
   $x \div 8 - 6 = 2$

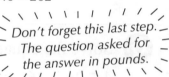

3) The width of a cuboid-shaped room is 3 m. The length of the room is four times the width of the room. The height of the room is y m. Which of these is the correct expression for finding the volume of the room in m³?
   A $12y \times 4$ **B** $3y \times 4y$ **C** $12y + 3y$ **D** $36y$ **E** $y + 36$

Volume of a cuboid is calculated by length × width × height.

Number Sequences

You need to follow the rule of a sequence to get from one number to the next.

Warm-Up Activity

What is the <u>difference</u> between <u>each number</u> in the sequence below?
See if you can work out what the <u>next number</u> in the sequence will be.

2   11   20   29   38

Some **Number Sequences** follow a **Pattern** you **Already Know**

1) You might <u>spot</u> a <u>pattern</u> in a <u>number sequence</u> because you recognise the numbers.

> 2, 3, 5, 7... — are all prime numbers going up in order.
> 25, 20, 15, 10... — are all multiples of 5 going down in order.
> 1, 4, 9, 16... — are all square numbers going up in order.

2) Once you know the <u>pattern</u> you can work out what the <u>next number</u> in the sequence will be.

> 1, 3, 5, 7... are all odd numbers going up in order. So the next number in the sequence will be 9.

3) You can also work out later numbers in the sequence. For example, to find the seventh number in this sequence of <u>odd numbers</u>, follow the <u>same pattern</u> until the seventh number.

> 1, 3, 5, 7, 9, 11, 13 — the seventh number in this sequence is 13.

You might need to **Find** the **Rule** for a **Number Sequence**

1) You might be given a <u>more difficult</u> number sequence, e.g. 4, 5, 7, 10, 14.

2) You'll need to work out the <u>rule</u> that the <u>number sequence</u> follows. One way to do this is to look at the <u>difference</u> between <u>each number</u> in the sequence.

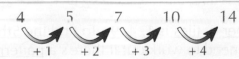

4   5   7   10   14
+ 1   + 2   + 3   + 4

The amount you need to add to get the next number in the sequence goes up by 1 each time. The next number in the sequence will be 14 + 5 = 19.

3) Make sure you look at <u>all</u> the values in the sequence when you're working out the rule. For example, the <u>start</u> of the sequence below looks like it follows the <u>same rule</u> as the one above — but if you look at <u>all</u> the values, you can see the rule is actually to <u>add</u> together the <u>previous two numbers</u> in the sequence:

> 2, 3, 5, 8, 13 ⟹ 2 + 3 = 5, 3 + 5 = 8, 5 + 8 = 13.

Section Three — Number Problems

The **Rule** for the **nth Term** helps you to find **Any Term**

1) You could be asked to find the <u>100th</u> or even the <u>1000th</u> term of a sequence. To find this you need to work out the rule for the <u>nth term</u>.

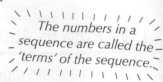
The numbers in a sequence are called the 'terms' of the sequence.

2) You use the nth term rule like a <u>formula</u> — substitute the term number for n to work out <u>what the term is</u>. For example, if the nth term rule was $8n + 1$, then the 100th term would be $8 \times 100 + 1 = 801$.

11+ *Style* Questions

> **Q** Scott made a sequence by starting from the number 14 and counting back in steps of 6. Which of these numbers is in Scott's sequence?
>
> A 4   B 1   C 0   D -2   E -4 ✓

Method

1) Write out the <u>number sequence</u> for this question and see which answer option is included in it.

Subtract 6 each time.

$$14 \xrightarrow{-6} 8 \xrightarrow{-6} 2 \xrightarrow{-6} -4$$

Writing out the sequence will help you avoid any mistakes.

2) Out of the options you're given, <u>only -4</u> appears in the <u>sequence</u>. So the answer is <u>E</u>.

> **Q** This triangle is made up of 9 small triangular tiles. It is three tiles high. In a larger triangle that is five tiles high, how many tiles would there be?

Method

1) You need to <u>find</u> what the <u>sequence</u> is.

→ If the shape is one tile high it has 1 tile. → △
→ If the shape is two tiles high it has 4 tiles. → ◭
→ If the shape is three tiles high it has 9 tiles. → ◭

2) So the <u>sequence</u> for the <u>number</u> of <u>tiles</u> is <u>1</u>, <u>4</u>, <u>9</u>. To find the <u>5th number</u> in this <u>sequence</u> you need to work out if there's a <u>pattern</u>.

3) The <u>difference</u> between each number in the sequence <u>increases by 2</u> each time — each row added has <u>two more tiles</u> than the last one. Now work out what the <u>5th number</u> in the <u>sequence</u> will be.

The difference increases by two each time, so apply this rule until you reach the 5th number.

$$1 \xrightarrow{+3} 4 \xrightarrow{+5} 9 \xrightarrow{+7} 16 \xrightarrow{+9} 25$$

4) If the shape was <u>five tiles high</u> it would have <u>25 tiles</u> in it.

Q Gael uses squares to make the first three terms of a sequence.

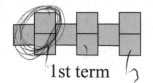 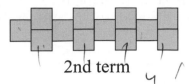 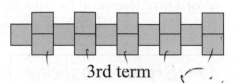

1st term $\quad$ 2nd term $\quad$ 3rd term

Write the expression for the number of squares in the nth term of the sequence.

─ **Method** ─────────────────────────────

If you have multiple choice options for a question like this, you could just test each option to see which expression works for the sequence.

1) Look for the relationship between the <u>number of squares</u> in each term.

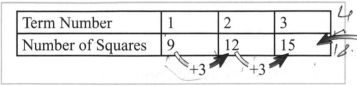

Term Number	1	2	3
Number of Squares	9	12	15

+3 $\quad$ +3

The number of squares increases by 3 between each term. The sequence is following the three times table, so you need to multiply by three in the expression.

2) <u>Start</u> your expression with '$3n$'.

For the 1st term, $n = 1$. So $3n = 3 \times 1 = 3$. The table says term 1 has 9 squares. So if you add 6, you have made a rule that works for the 1st term of the sequence, $3n + 6$.

3) Check your expression is <u>correct</u> by testing the <u>other terms</u>.

For the 2nd term, $3n + 6 = 3 \times 2 + 6 = 12$. For the 3rd term, $3n + 6 = 3 \times 3 + 6 = 15$.

4) The expression works for <u>all three terms</u>. So the correct answer is <u>$3n + 6$</u>.

Practice Questions

1) Jake is building a wall. He lays four bricks in the first hour, 5 in the second and 6 in the third. Each hour he continues to add one more brick than he laid in the previous hour. How many bricks will he have laid after 6 hours?

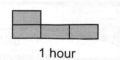 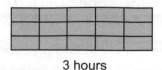

1 hour $\qquad$ 2 hours $\qquad$ 3 hours

2) Here is a sequence of numbers.

$$7 \quad 12 \quad 17 \quad 22 \quad 27$$

Write the expression for the nth term of this sequence.

Word Problems

Word problems can be tricky — you need to read them very carefully to work out what they're asking. Then you can work out the best way to answer them quickly and correctly.

 Q A zoo has a total of 39 parrots and peacocks.
Which of these statements cannot be true?

A There are more parrots than peacocks in the zoo.
B There are more peacocks than parrots in the zoo.
C There are three more parrots than peacocks in the zoo.
D There are seven more peacocks than parrots in the zoo.
E There are twelve more parrots than peacocks in the zoo.

Method 1

1) Try to find a <u>pair of numbers</u> that works for each statement.

A	For example, there could be 20 parrots and 19 peacocks — so this could be true.
B	For example, there could be 20 peacocks and 19 parrots — so this could be true.
C	For example, there could be 21 parrots and 18 peacocks — so this could be true.
D	For example, there could be 23 peacocks and 16 parrots — so this could be true.
E	There isn't a pair of whole numbers that differ by twelve and add up to 39 — so this cannot be true.

2) The correct answer is <u>option E</u>.

Method 2

1) Use your knowledge of <u>odd</u> and <u>even</u> numbers to work out which statement <u>cannot</u> be true.

2) The total number of birds is odd, which means the <u>sum</u> of the number of parrots and peacocks must be an <u>odd</u> number <u>added</u> to an <u>even</u> number.

3) The difference between an odd and an even number is always <u>odd</u> — so <u>option E</u> cannot be true as the difference between the number of birds is <u>even</u>.

4) The total number of birds is odd, so there must be <u>more</u> of one type of bird than the other. So <u>either</u> statement A <u>or</u> statement B <u>could</u> be true — but there <u>isn't enough information</u> in the question to work out which.

5) The correct answer is <u>option E</u>.

Beanthwaite School ordered 6 boxes of rulers in March and 4 boxes in April.
Each box contained 130 rulers.
How many rulers did the school order in total?

Method

1) Work out the <u>total number</u> of <u>boxes</u> ordered.

> 6 boxes were ordered in March and 4 were ordered in April, so 6 + 4 = 10.

2) <u>Multiply</u> the total number of boxes by the <u>number</u> of <u>rulers</u> in each box.

> 10 × 130 = 1300 rulers in total.

 Raisa went to a restaurant with two friends.
They ordered from the menu: 3 plates of
lasagne, 2 soups and 4 lemonades.

Raisa paid with a £50 note.

How much change did she receive?

> **Luigi's Restaurant**
>
> Lemonade................ 90p
> Soup......................£2.50
> Carbonara..............£7.50
> Pizza.....................£6.00
> Lasagne.................£8.50

Method

1) Work out how much <u>each item</u> will <u>cost</u>. Make sure that all the amounts are in <u>pounds</u>.

> 3 plates of lasagne is 3 × £8.50.   2 soups is 2 × £2.50.   4 lemonades is 4 × 90p.
> Split £8.50 into £8 and £0.50   2 × £2.50 = £5.00   4 × 90p = 360p
> 3 × £8 = £24, 3 × £0.50 = £1.50   360p = £3.60
> So 3 × £8.50 = £24 + £1.50 = £25.50

2) Now find the <u>total cost</u> of <u>all</u> of the <u>items</u>.

> You could use partitioning to find the total amount.
> Add up all the pounds. 25 + 5 + 3 = £33.
> Add up all the pence. 50 + 60 = 110p = £1.10
> Now add them together. £33 + £1.10 = £34.10

For questions like this where you have lots of numbers to work with, it's helpful to make notes on any rough paper you are given.

3) Now find the <u>difference</u> between the <u>total cost</u> of the <u>items</u> and <u>£50</u>.

> You can count on from £34.10 to £50.
> Count on to £35. £34.10 + 90p = £35
> Then count on to £50. £35 + £15 = £50
> Add the two numbers to find the difference. £15 + 90p = £15.90.

4) So the <u>answer</u> is <u>£15.90</u>.

Q I am thinking of a positive number.
If I multiply it by 3, then square it, I get 36.
What number am I thinking of?

   A 2   B 4   C 6   D 8   E 10

Method

You know the <u>final answer</u> — to find the <u>number at the start</u> you need to work
<u>backwards</u> through the calculation given in the question. You can do this in <u>two steps</u>.

> 1) The number at the end is 36. To get 36 a number was squared.
>   The only positive number that could be squared to give 36 is 6.

> 2) To get 6 a number was multiplied by 3.
>   To find this number you just divide 6 by 3. $6 \div 3 = 2$.

Q A drinks company makes 250 litres of tropical
punch each week. Look at the ingredients
used to make the punch.

The company sells the tropical
punch in 50-litre barrels.

Tropical Punch	
Mango Juice	95.4 litres
Orange Juice	45.5 litres
Pineapple Juice	62.1 litres
Apple Juice	47 litres

How many litres of orange juice are in one barrel of tropical punch?

   A 3.4 litres   C 18.0 litres   E 11.6 litres
   B 8.5 litres   D 9.1 litres

Method

1) First you need to work out what <u>fraction</u> of <u>250 litres</u> makes up <u>1 barrel</u> of <u>tropical punch</u>.

> 1 barrel = 50 litres. $250 \div 50 = 5$, so 1 barrel is $\frac{1}{5}$ of 250 litres.

2) There are <u>45.5 litres</u> of orange juice in <u>250 litres</u> of tropical punch,
    so you need to find $\frac{1}{5}$ of 45.5 litres.

> To find $\frac{1}{5}$ of 45.5 you need to divide 45.5 by 5.
>
> There are options to choose from, so you could make an estimate.
> $45 \div 5 = 9$, so the answer to $45.5 \div 5$ will be a little greater than 9.
> Option D is 9.1 litres — so this is the correct answer.

Q A counter is worth 5 points and has a diameter of 3.5 cm.
A row of counters was lined up along a wall, with each counter
touching the next. The values on the line of counters added up
to 1500 points.

Find the length of the row of
counters, in metres.

3.5 cm

Method

1) Work out how many <u>counters</u> there are in <u>total</u>.

> There are 1500 points worth of 5 point counters.
> So the total number of counters is 1500 ÷ 5.
> 1500 is 100 times larger than 15, so 1500 ÷ 5 must be 100 times larger than 15 ÷ 5.
> 15 ÷ 5 = 3. So 1500 ÷ 5 = 100 × 3 = 300

2) Now find the <u>length</u> of the <u>line</u> of <u>counters</u>.

> Each counter is 3.5 cm in diameter, and there are 300 in total — so work out 300 × 3.5.
> Partition 3.5 into 3 and 0.5:
> 300 × 3 = 900
> 300 × 0.5 = 150 (it's the same as half of 300).
> Then add up the result:
> 900 + 150 = 1050 cm.

3) Don't forget to <u>convert</u> your <u>answer</u> into <u>metres</u>: <u>1050 cm</u> ÷ 100 = <u>10.5 m</u>.

Practice Questions

1) A bunch of seven tulips costs £4.50. A bunch of six roses costs £3.50.
Lena wants 42 tulips and 42 roses. How much does she need to pay?

A £24.50
B £147.00
C £189.00
D £27.00
E £51.50

2) Benni buys 5 sandwiches that all cost the same amount. He pays with
a £10 note and gets £1.50 change. How much is one sandwich?

3) Simone made bracelets to sell. Each bracelet cost her 20p to make and
she sold them for 50p each. She sold 57 bracelets in total. How much
money did she make, after she subtracted the cost of making the bracelets?

Data Tables

Data is just any facts or information. It's often easier to understand and use if you organise it into a table, particularly if there's a lot of it.

Warm-Up Activity

Roll a dice 30 times. Record the number you roll in a frequency table like the one on the right. How many times did you roll each number?

Number on dice	Tally	Frequency
1	IIII	4
2	⊔Π I	6
3	IΠ	5

Frequency just means how many times something happens.

11+ Style Questions

Q Ryan does a survey to find out how much the shops in his town charge for a can of cola. He groups his results into price bands and puts them in this table.
Which of these statements is definitely true?

Price	Frequency
50p – 59p	4
60p – 69p	10
70p – 79p	12
80p – 89p	8
90p – £1.00	6

A The most expensive can of cola Ryan found costs £1.00.

B Ryan recorded the prices of 42 cans of cola.

C More than half of the cans of cola cost between 70p and 79p each.

D Three-quarters of the cans of cola cost less than 80p each.

E More than half of the cans of cola cost 70p or more each.

Method

Look at each option and work out whether it's definitely true.

A The table only tells you that the most expensive can of cola is between 90p and £1.00. It might not be exactly £1.00 though — so you don't know if the statement is definitely true.

B To find the total number of cans of cola, add up all the frequencies in the table. $4 + 10 + 12 + 8 + 6 = 40$ — so the statement isn't true.

C Half of the total number of cans is $40 \div 2 = 20$. There are only 12 cola cans in the 70p –79p price band — so the statement isn't true.

D One-quarter of the total number of cans is $40 \div 4 = 10$, so three-quarters is 30. Add together the first three rows to find the number of cans that cost less than 80p: $4 + 10 + 12 = 26$. 26 isn't three-quarters of the total number of cans — so the statement isn't true.

E Add together the last three rows of the table to find the total number of cans that cost 70p or more $= 12 + 8 + 6 = 26$. This is more than half of the total number of cans (20) — so this statement is true. E is the correct answer.

Q Years 5 and 6 are having a party. They all choose between meat pie and cheese pie. This table shows some of their choices. How many children are there in Year 5?

	Year 5	Year 6	Total
Meat pie	13	12	25
Cheese pie	21	018	39
Total			64

Method

1) This is a <u>two-way table</u>. There's a total for each row and column.

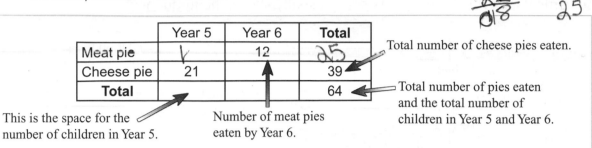

	Year 5	Year 6	Total
Meat pie		12	25
Cheese pie	21		39
Total			64

Total number of cheese pies eaten.

Total number of pies eaten and the total number of children in Year 5 and Year 6.

This is the space for the number of children in Year 5.

Number of meat pies eaten by Year 6.

$$39 \quad \quad 64$$
$$-21 \quad \quad -39$$
$$018 \quad \quad 25$$

2) You don't have enough <u>information</u> to work out how many children there are in Year 5 straight away — you need to <u>fill in</u> some of the other <u>empty</u> boxes first.

	Year 5	Year 6	Total
Meat pie	**13**	12	**25**
Cheese pie	21		39
Total			64

First find out how many meat pies were eaten in total.
Total number – total cheese pie eaters = 64 – 39 = 25

Now you can find out how many meat pies Year 5 ate.
Total meat pie eaters – Year 6 meat pie eaters = 25 – 12 = 13

3) <u>Add</u> the numbers in the <u>Year 5 column</u> of the table to find the number of children in Year 5.

Year 5 children = Year 5 meat + Year 5 cheese
pie eaters   pie eaters

= 13 + 21 = 34

	Year 5	Year 6	Total
Meat pie	**13**	12	25
Cheese pie	21		39
Total	**34**		64

Practice Questions

1) The table on the right shows the numbers of DVDs owned by some children. How many children own more than 15 DVDs?

A 9   **B** 19   C 28   D 27   E 13

DVDs	Frequency
0 – 5	14
6 – 10	13
11 – 15	9
16 – 20	13
21 – 25	6

2) The table below shows an order form for some pantomime tickets. Some boxes have been left empty. Calculate the cost of a senior citizen ticket.

Ticket	Price	Number needed	Total cost
Child	£5	32	£160
Adult	£8	4	£32
Senior Citizen	£6	3	£18
		Booking Fee	£2.50
		Amount to pay	£212.50

192
-202.5
£19 45

Displaying Data

Charts and graphs aren't just an excuse for a bit of colouring. They're a really important way of showing data — they can help you understand information at a glance.

Bar Charts Make it Easy to Compare things

Bar charts have two axes. The horizontal axis is called the x-axis. The vertical axis is called the y-axis — it usually shows the frequency.

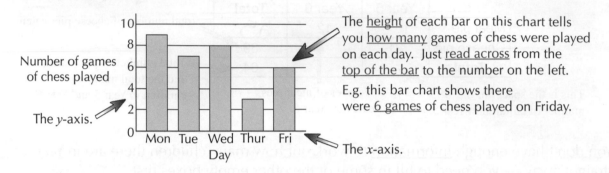

The height of each bar on this chart tells you how many games of chess were played on each day. Just read across from the top of the bar to the number on the left.

E.g. this bar chart shows there were 6 games of chess played on Friday.

The y-axis.

The x-axis.

Line Graphs Often Show things that Change over Time

1) Line graphs show you how one thing (shown on the y-axis) changes as another thing changes (shown on the x-axis).

2) Time is often on the x-axis. For example, this graph shows how the temperature in an oven changes over time.

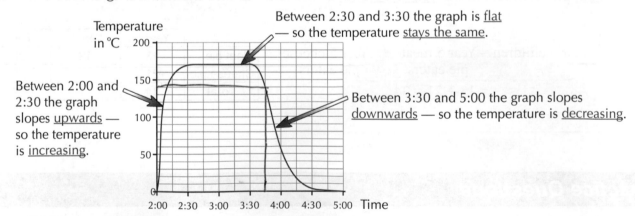

Between 2:30 and 3:30 the graph is flat — so the temperature stays the same.

Between 2:00 and 2:30 the graph slopes upwards — so the temperature is increasing.

Between 3:30 and 5:00 the graph slopes downwards — so the temperature is decreasing.

3) Here's how to read off a value from a line graph, e.g. the temperature at 3:45 from this line graph.

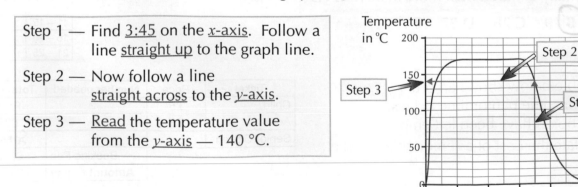

Step 1 — Find 3:45 on the x-axis. Follow a line straight up to the graph line.

Step 2 — Now follow a line straight across to the y-axis.

Step 3 — Read the temperature value from the y-axis — 140 °C.

Section Four — Data Handling

Pictograms use Symbols to Show Frequency

1) In pictograms, simple pictures show numbers of things or how often something happens.

2) The key is really important — it tells you how many things each picture stands for.

This pictogram shows how many chess games were played each day.

This is the key. It tells you that one complete symbol represents 2 games.

♟ = 2 games of chess

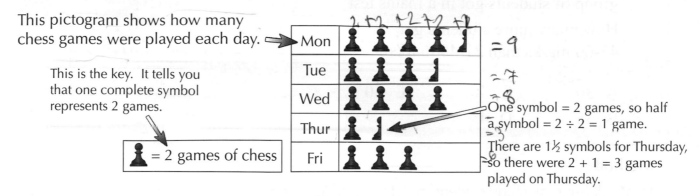

Mon	♟♟♟♟♟ = 9
Tue	♟♟♟♟ ~7
Wed	♟♟♟♟ ~8
Thur	♟♟ =3
Fri	♟♟♟ 6

One symbol = 2 games, so half a symbol = 2 ÷ 2 = 1 game. There are 1½ symbols for Thursday, so there were 2 + 1 = 3 games played on Thursday.

Pie Charts Show Things as Proportions

Proportion just means the fraction of the total amount.

1) Each 'slice' of a pie chart is called a sector. You can work out the number of things shown by each sector on a pie chart.

2) For example, the pie chart below shows what 60 four-year-old boys said they wanted to be when they grow up. You can find how many boys said each thing by working out what fraction a sector is of the whole pie.

total = 60

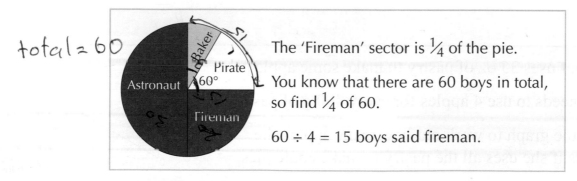

The 'Fireman' sector is ¼ of the pie.

You know that there are 60 boys in total, so find ¼ of 60.

60 ÷ 4 = 15 boys said fireman.

You can also use the number of degrees that make up a sector to work out how many boys said each thing.

The 'Pirate' sector has an angle of 60°.

The pie chart is a circle, so the total angle of all the sectors is 360°.

The fraction of the whole pie made up by the pirate sector is $\frac{60°}{360°} = \frac{1}{6}$ (÷ 60)

So the number of boys that want to be a pirate is ⅙ of 60 = 60 ÷ 6 = 10.

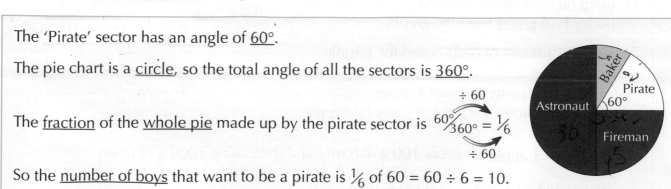

11+ *Style* Questions

Q The bar chart shows the scores a year group of students got in a maths test.

How many more students got 41-60 marks than 21-40 marks?

A 30   C 40   E 50
B 35   D 45

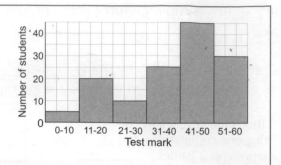

Method

1) Work out how many students got <u>41-60 marks</u>, and how many students got <u>21-40 marks</u>.

| 41-50 bar = 45 students |
| 51-60 bar = 30 students |
| 45 + 30 = 75 students got 41-60 marks. |

| 21-30 bar = 10 students |
| 31-40 bar = 25 students |
| 10 + 25 = 35 students got 21-40 marks. |

2) <u>Subtract</u> the number of students who got 21-40 marks from the number who got 41-60 marks.

| 75 − 35 = 40 students |

3) The answer is <u>option C</u> — <u>40 students</u>.

Q A chef uses 35 oz of pastry to make some apple pies.

She needs to use 4 apples for every 400 g of pastry.

Use the graph to work out how many apples she needs if she uses all the pastry to make apple pies.

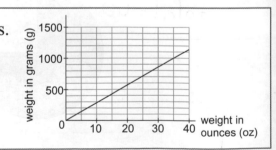

Method

1) <u>Read off</u> how much 35 oz of pastry is <u>in grams</u> from the graph.

35 oz = 1000 g. ⟶

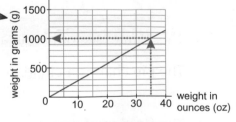

2) Find the amount of pastry used for <u>1 apple</u>.

| For 400 g of pastry you need 4 apples. |
| So she uses 400 ÷ 4 = 100 g of pastry for 1 apple. |

3) She needs <u>1 apple</u> for every <u>100 g</u> of pastry and she's using <u>1000 g</u> of pastry.

| 1000 ÷ 100 = 10 — she needs 10 apples. |

Section Four — Data Handling

Q The pictogram shows the number of differently shaped sweets in a bag.

How many more animal shaped sweets than fruit shaped sweets are there in the bag?

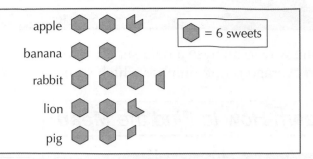

Method

1) First work out <u>how many</u> sweets are <u>animal shaped</u> (i.e. either a rabbit, a lion or a pig).

> There are 7 whole symbols for the animal sweets. $7 \times 6 = 42$ sweets.
> The rabbit shape also has $\frac{3}{6}$ of a symbol on the end = 3 sweets, the lion shape has $\frac{4}{6}$ of a symbol on the end = 4 sweets and the pig shape has $\frac{2}{6}$ of a symbol on the end = 2 sweets.
> Add these together to get the total number of animal shaped sweets. $42 + 3 + 4 + 2 = 51$ sweets.

2) Now use the same method to work out <u>how many fruit shaped sweets</u> there are.

> There are 4 whole symbols for fruit shaped sweets. $4 \times 6 = 24$ sweets. The apple shape also has $\frac{5}{6}$ of a symbol on the end = 5 sweets. Total number of fruit shaped sweets = $24 + 5 = 29$ sweets.

3) Then <u>subtract</u> to find the <u>difference</u> between the two.

> There are $51 - 29 = 22$ more animal shaped sweets than fruit shaped sweets.

Q The table shows the ingredients in 300 ml of a salad dressing. Ben wants to draw a pie chart to show the proportion of each ingredient in the dressing.

What angle would the olive oil sector of the pie chart have?

Ingredient	Amount
Olive oil	50 ml
Vinegar	200 ml
Lemon juice	50 ml

Method

1) First find what <u>fraction</u> of the dressing is made up of olive oil.

> 50 ml out of 300 ml is olive oil.
> The fraction of the total dressing that's olive oil is $\frac{50}{300} = \frac{1}{6}$
>
>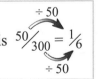
>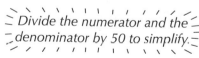
> *Divide the numerator and the denominator by 50 to simplify.*

2) The <u>total angles</u> in a pie chart are <u>360°</u>, so find $\frac{1}{6}$ of 360°.

> $\frac{1}{6}$ of 360° = 360° ÷ 6 = 60°.

Practice Question

1) A class of children were asked what their favourite colour is.
   Two children chose brown. This was represented on a pie chart
   by a 20° sector. How many children are in the class?

Analysing Data

One way to analyse a data set is calculate the mean, a type of average.
An average is one number which summarises a whole set of numbers.

Learn How to Find the *Mean*

The *Mean* Involves *Adding* and *Dividing*

1) To work out the <u>mean</u>: ⟶
   - <u>Add</u> up all the numbers in the data set.
   - <u>Divide</u> the total by <u>how many</u> numbers there are.

2) So to work out the mean of the data set on the <u>right</u>, first add up all the numbers:
   13 + 8 + 7 + 4 + 11 + 2 = 45.

   | 13, 8, 7, 4, 11, 2 |

3) There are six numbers, so divide the total by six: 45 ÷ 6 = 7.5.

11+ *Style* Questions

Q Marcus works on a stall that sells fruit smoothies.
The table below shows the price of each type of smoothie.

Banana	£2.70
Mango	£3.10
Strawberry	£2.50
Raspberry	£2.70

What is the mean price of a smoothie from Marcus's stall?

Method

1) <u>Add</u> together the prices of all the smoothies.

   £2.70 + £3.10 + £2.50 + £2.70 = £11

2) There are four different types of smoothie, so <u>divide</u> the total by <u>four</u>.

   The mean price of a smoothie is £11 ÷ 4 = £2.75

Q The bar chart shows five children's marks in three tests.

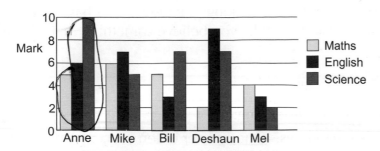

Which child had the highest mean mark across all the tests?

Method

1) <u>Add</u> together each child's marks and <u>divide</u> them by <u>three</u> to find each mean mark.

Anne: $(5 + 6 + 10) \div 3 = 7$ Mike: $(6 + 7 + 5) \div 3 = 6$ Bill: $(5 + 3 + 7) \div 3 = 5$
Deshaun: $(2 + 9 + 7) \div 3 = 6$ Mel: $(4 + 3 + 2) \div 3 = 3$

2) <u>Compare</u> the means — the highest is 7, so the answer is Anne.

Q Derek has a set of five numbers. He calculates that the mean of his numbers is 11.5.

| 8 | 13 | 18 | 7.5 | 11 |

He forgets one of his numbers.
The mean of the four numbers he can remember is 12.5.

Which number has he forgotten?

Method

1) First work out the <u>total</u> of the numbers <u>he can remember</u>.

If the mean of the four numbers he can remember is 12.5, he must have divided a number by 4 to get 12.5. So multiply 12.5 by 4 to find the total. $12.5 \times 4 = 50$.

2) Then work out the <u>total</u> of the <u>original five numbers</u>.

$8 + 13 + 18 + 7.5 + 11 = 57.5$

3) <u>Subtract</u> the total of the four numbers he can <u>remember</u> from the <u>original total</u>.

$57.5 - 50 = 7.5$ — the number he forgot was 7.5.

Practice Question

1) The data set on the right shows how many tea bags were used in the Smith household each day. What was the mean number of tea bags used per day?

Mon	Tue	Wed	Thur	Fri
22	23	17	17	26

Section Four — Data Handling

Misleading Data

People often use data to try to prove a point they're making. However, you have to think really hard about data to make sure it's not being twisted to make you believe something that's not true.

See if you can spot why this statement is <u>misleading</u>:

Sprouts are <u>more popular</u> with girls than boys. <u>One-quarter</u> of ten year old girls <u>like</u> sprouts, whereas <u>75%</u> of ten year old boys <u>don't like</u> them.

11+ Style Questions

Children prefer playing computer games to playing sport.

A group of school children were asked, 'What is your favourite weekend activity?'. 20% of them said 'playing computer games', while only 1 in 4 children said their favourite activity was 'playing sport'.

Why is this newspaper article misleading?

A   The article doesn't say what other activities the children picked.

B   According to the numbers given in the article, more children said they liked playing sport than playing computer games.

C   The article doesn't tell you how many boys and girls were in the group asked.

D   The figures in the article show that fewer children chose sport than computer games.

E   The article doesn't tell you what sports or computer games the children like to play.

Method

1) <u>Read the article</u> and work out what the article is <u>claiming</u> to be <u>true</u>.

> The headline says that children prefer playing computer games to playing sport.

2) Look <u>carefully</u> at any <u>figures</u> you're given, to see if they <u>back up</u> what the article is <u>claiming</u>. Put the figures into the <u>same form</u> (e.g. fractions, decimals or percentages) to <u>compare</u> them.

> 20% of children said their favourite activity was playing computer games.
> 1 in 4 children said playing sport — which is the same as 25%.
>
> 25% is greater than 20%, so more children said playing sport than playing computer games.

3) Look at the <u>options</u> to see which one is <u>correct</u>.

> Options A, C, and E are all true, but they don't mean that the article is misleading.
> Option D is incorrect — the figures show that more children chose sport than computer games.
> Option B is correct. The article is misleading because it says that fewer people picked sport than computer games, when the figures show that more people picked sport than computer games.

Q This graph is used to show the increase in the number of chickens eaten by the population of a country between 2010 and 2011.

Why is the graph misleading?

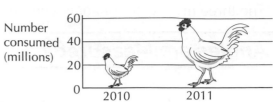

A Only two years are shown on the graph.
B The scale on the vertical axis is uneven.
C The graph doesn't show how many turkeys were eaten.
D We are not told which country the data is about.
E The chicken picture for 2011 is more than double the area of the 2010 picture.

Method

1) The graph is a type of bar chart, but it uses <u>pictures</u> of chickens instead of bars.
The <u>height</u> of each picture tells you how many chickens were eaten.

> It shows that 30 million chickens were eaten in 2010, and 60 million chickens were eaten in 2011.

2) Look at each answer and decide if it's a <u>good reason</u> why the graph is misleading.

> A: The graph is only about 2010 and 2011, so it's not misleading that only two years are shown.
> B: This isn't true. The values are evenly spaced.
> C: It doesn't matter how many turkeys are eaten — the graph is about chickens.
> D: You haven't been led to believe that the data is about anywhere in particular, so this isn't the answer.
> E: From reading the graph you know that about twice as many chickens were eaten in 2011 than 2010.
> The trouble is, the area of the chicken for 2011 is about 4 times as big as the area of the chicken for 2010. This means that at a glance, the graph makes it look like many more chickens got eaten in 2011 compared to 2010 than actually were. E is the correct answer.

Tips and Tricks for Misleading Data questions

Watch out for graphs that have a y-axis that doesn't start at zero (shown by a zigzag line).

E.g. These bar charts show the same data, but the second one makes the difference in the heights of the bars look much bigger than the first.

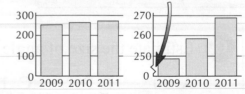

Practice Question

1) A newspaper report with a graph has the headline:
Sales of pencils plummet. Why is the report misleading?

A There are no crosses on the graph to mark the plotted points.
B The graph does not show how many pens were sold.
C The y-axis doesn't start on zero so it makes the drop in sales look worse than it is.
D The graph doesn't show what happened before 2002.
E The pencil manufacturers want you to go and buy more pencils.

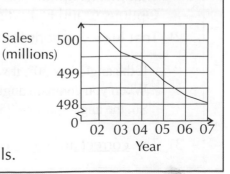

Section Four — Data Handling

Angles

The three main types of angle you need to learn are right angles, acute angles and obtuse angles.

Angles are Measured using Degrees (°)

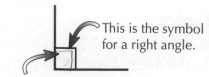
This is the symbol for a right angle.

Right angles measure exactly 90°.

Acute angles measure between 0 and 90°.

Obtuse angles measure between 90° and 180°.

Learn these Rules about Angles

Angles around a Point Add Up to 360°

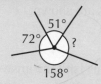

The four angles total 360°.
So the missing angle is
360 − 51 − 72 − 158 = 79°.

Angles on a Straight Line Add Up to 180°

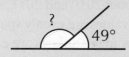

The two angles total 180°.
So the missing angle is
180 − 49 = 131°.

Angles in a Triangle Add Up to 180°

The three angles total 180°.
So the missing angle is
180 − 74 − 74 = 32°.

Angles in a Quadrilateral Add Up to 360°

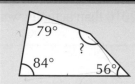

The four angles total 360°.
So the missing angle is
360 − 84 − 79 − 56 = 141°.

11+ Style Questions

Q Estimate the size of angle x.

    A 90°   **B** 30°   **C** 105°   **D** 75°   **E** 120°

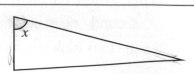

Method

1) It's <u>smaller than 90°</u>, so it must be an <u>acute</u> angle.
   That means option A is <u>incorrect</u> — it's a right angle.
   Options C and E are also <u>incorrect</u> — they're <u>obtuse</u> angles.

You can't do a calculation here — you don't know the sizes of the other angles.

2) That leaves options B and D. You need to decide which option is <u>more realistic</u>.

> If the angle was 30°, it would be three times smaller than a right angle.
> When you compare angle x to a right angle, it's only a little bit smaller.
> So, the angle must be 75° — it's the most realistic option.

You can compare an unknown angle with a right angle using the corner of a sheet of paper.

3) The <u>correct answer</u> is option <u>D</u> — 75°.

Q What is the size of the angle marked *a* between the two hands on this clock?

$$\frac{360\ ?}{12}$$

30

Method

1) The <u>total angle</u> around the centre point of the clock is <u>360°</u>.

2) There are <u>12 hours</u> equally spaced apart on the clock.
   Work out the size of the angle <u>between each hour</u>.

   Divide the total angle ⟶ $360 \div 12 = 30°$ ⟶ The angle between each
   by the number of hours.   hour on the clock is 30°.

3) Work out <u>how many hours</u> apart the two hands are.

   > The minute hand is at 12 and the hour hand is at 5. They are 5 hours apart.

4) <u>Multiply</u> the <u>number of hours</u> by <u>30°</u> to find the value of the missing angle.

   > $5 \times 30 = 150°$. Angle *a* is 150°.

Q Ted made the following pattern using a rectangle and a triangle. What is the size of angle *x*?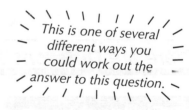

Method

1) Work out the <u>size</u> of the other angle in the triangle.

 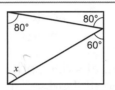 Angles on a straight line add up to 180°.

   The angle is $180 - 80 - 60 = 40°$.

   This is one of several different ways you could work out the answer to this question.

2) The three angles in a <u>triangle</u> add up to <u>180°</u>. Use this rule to work out the size of *x*:

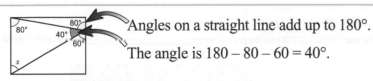 You have two angles of the triangle. Their total is $80 + 40 = 120°$.

   Angle *x* is the third angle in the triangle. It is $180 - 120 = 60°$.

Practice Questions

1) Estimate the size of angle *c*.
     A 100°   **B** 125°   **C** 10°   **D** 45°   **E** 90°

2) What is the size of the angle between the north east and south points on this compass?

   Think about the total number of points on the compass.

2D Shapes

2D shapes are flat — they have a length and a width but no depth.

Quadrilaterals *are shapes with* Four Sides

Make sure that you know the properties of these quadrilaterals.

Parallel lines have exactly the same slope.

Square
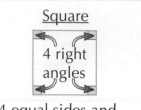
4 right angles

4 equal sides and
2 pairs of parallel sides

Trapezium
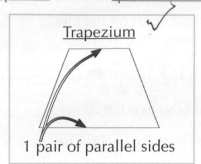
1 pair of parallel sides

Rectangle
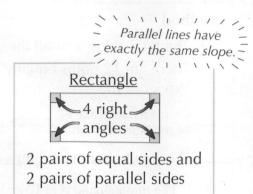
4 right angles

2 pairs of equal sides and
2 pairs of parallel sides

Parallelogram
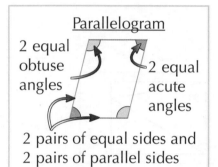
2 equal obtuse angles

2 equal acute angles

2 pairs of equal sides and
2 pairs of parallel sides

Kite
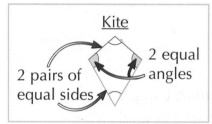
2 pairs of equal sides

2 equal angles

Rhombus
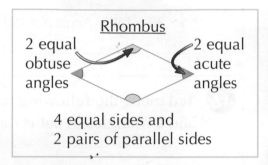
2 equal obtuse angles

2 equal acute angles

4 equal sides and
2 pairs of parallel sides

There are Different Types *of* Triangle

The angles in a triangle add up to 180° (see page 56).

1) Equilateral *Triangle*
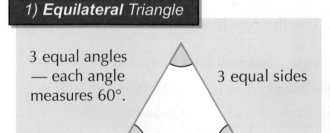
3 equal angles — each angle measures 60°.

3 equal sides

2) Isosceles *Triangle*
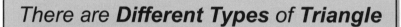
2 equal sides

2 equal angles

3) Scalene *Triangle*
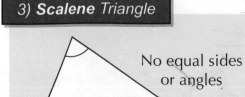
No equal sides or angles

4) Right-angled *Triangle*
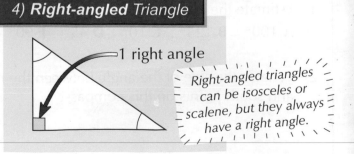
1 right angle

Right-angled triangles can be isosceles or scalene, but they always have a right angle.

Regular Polygons *have* Equal Sides *and* Angles

A polygon is a 2D shape with straight sides.

<u>Regular Pentagon</u>

5 equal sides and
5 equal angles

<u>Regular Hexagon</u>

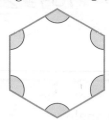

6 equal sides and
6 equal angles

<u>Regular Heptagon</u>

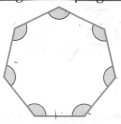

7 equal sides and
7 equal angles

<u>Regular Octagon</u>

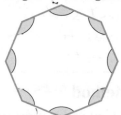

8 equal sides and
8 equal angles

<u>Irregular</u> polygons have <u>at least one</u> side or angle that's <u>different</u> in size. E.g. an <u>irregular</u> <u>pentagon</u> has five sides but at least one of the sides or angles is different from the others.

11+ *Style* Questions

Q Which of the following shapes should be placed in area Z of the Venn diagram?

A Square
B Rectangle
C Rhombus
D Isosceles Triangle
E Trapezium

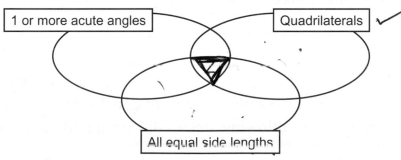

1 or more acute angles

Quadrilaterals ✓

All equal side lengths

Method

1) Area Z is in the <u>centre</u> of the Venn diagram. You need to find the option that's a <u>quadrilateral</u> with <u>1 or more acute angles</u> and <u>all equal side lengths</u>.

2) First, eliminate any options that <u>aren't quadrilaterals</u>.

> An isosceles triangle has 3 sides so it's not a quadrilateral. The answer isn't option D.

3) Next, eliminate the options that <u>don't have all equal side lengths</u>.

> Rectangles and trapeziums don't have all equal side lengths. The answer isn't option B or E.

4) That leaves <u>A</u> and <u>C</u>. Eliminate the option that <u>doesn't</u> have <u>1 or more acute angles</u>.

> A square has 4 right angles. The answer isn't option A.

5) The correct answer must be a <u>rhombus</u> — <u>option C</u>.
It's a quadrilateral with 2 acute angles and 4 equal sides.

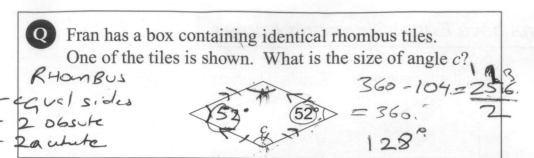

Q Fran has a box containing identical rhombus tiles.
One of the tiles is shown. What is the size of angle *c*?

Handwritten: RHOMBUS
- equal sides
- 2 obsute
- 2 acute

Handwritten: 360 - 104 = 256
= 360
128°

Handwritten: 256 / 2

─ **Method** ────────────────────────────────

1) Start by working out the size of the <u>other acute angle</u>.

> A rhombus has two equal acute
> angles. So, this angle is also 52°.

There's more about acute angles and obtuse angles on page 56.

2) Work out the <u>total size</u> of the two <u>obtuse angles</u>.

> A rhombus is a quadrilateral, so the total size of the angles is 360°.
> This means that the total size of the two remaining angles is 360 − 52 − 52 = 256°.

3) You can now calculate the size of <u>angle *c*</u>.

> A rhombus has two equal obtuse angles,
> so the size of angle *c* is 256° ÷ 2 = 128°.

───

Q Tariq put five shapes into a bag. He pulled one out at random.
The shape had exactly one <u>pair of equal sides</u>, <u>no parallel</u> sides and no obtuse angles.
Which of the following shapes did Tariq pull out of the bag?

 **A**   **B**   **C**   **D** 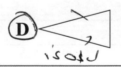   **E**

Handwritten: isosl

─ **Method** ────────────────────────────────

1) Work through <u>each option</u> until you find the one that <u>matches</u> the <u>description</u> of the shape.

> Option A has one pair of parallel sides so it's incorrect.

> Option B has five equal sides and five obtuse angles so it's incorrect.

> Option C has two pairs of equal sides and two obtuse angles so it's incorrect.

> Option D has one pair of equal sides, no parallel sides and no obtuse angles.

2) <u>Option D</u> matches the description of the shape that Tariq chose — this is the <u>correct</u> answer.

3) You can <u>check</u> option E to make sure you haven't made a <u>mistake</u>.

> Option E has four equal sides, two pairs of parallel sides and two obtuse angles so it's incorrect.

Section Five — Shape and Space

Q Which shape should go in the grey box of the sorting table?

A Regular hexagon
B Equilateral triangle
C Regular pentagon
D Parallelogram
E Rectangle

	At least one obtuse angle	No obtuse angles
All sides equal lengths	*Rhombus*	*B*
Exactly two pairs of equal length sides		

Method

1) First rule out the shapes that <u>don't fit</u> in the 'at least one obtuse angle' <u>column</u>.

> Equilateral triangles and rectangles don't have any obtuse angles so you can rule out B and E.

2) Then rule out the shapes that <u>don't fit</u> in the 'two pairs of equal length sides' <u>row</u>.

> Regular hexagons and regular pentagons both have all equal length sides — you can rule out A and C.

3) So, the only shape that fits in the '<u>at least one obtuse angle</u>' column and the '<u>two pairs of equal length sides</u>' row is a parallelogram. The correct answer is <u>option D</u>.

Practice Questions

1) Rhona is describing a triangular tile to her friends. She says that it has no right angles, no equal sides and no equal angles. What is the shape of the tile that Rhona is describing?
   A Equilateral triangle   B Isosceles triangle   C Scalene triangle   D Right-angled triangle

2) Which shape should go in the grey box of the sorting table?

   A Trapezium
   B Square
   C Rectangle
   D Equilateral triangle
   E Rhombus

	All equal angles	Angles aren't all equal
All equal side lengths		
Side lengths aren't all equal		

3) Naomi is thinking of a shape. She gives David some clues about it:
   - The shape has no obtuse angles.
   - The shape has no right angles.
   - Two of its sides are equal in length.

   What shape is Naomi thinking of?

Section Five — Shape and Space

2D Shapes — Perimeter and Area

The length around the edge of a shape is its perimeter. The space covered by a shape is its area.

Warm-Up Activity

1) <u>Measure</u> one of the short and one of the long <u>edges</u> of a book cover using a <u>ruler</u>.
2) Use the measurements to try to work out the <u>perimeter</u> and <u>area</u> of the book cover.

Perimeter is the **Length Around** *a* **Shape**

1) To calculate the <u>perimeter</u> of a shape, <u>add up</u> the length of <u>every side</u> of the shape.

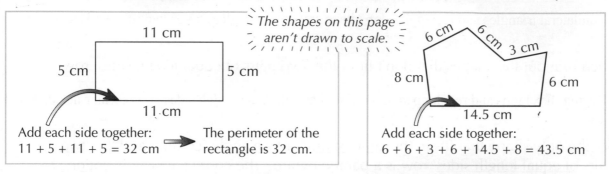

The shapes on this page aren't drawn to scale.

Add each side together:
11 + 5 + 11 + 5 = 32 cm → The perimeter of the rectangle is 32 cm.

Add each side together:
6 + 6 + 3 + 6 + 14.5 + 8 = 43.5 cm

2) Sometimes you <u>don't know</u> the length of every side. You need to <u>work out</u> the missing lengths.

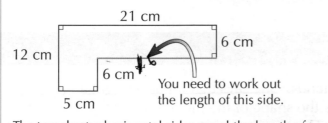

You need to work out the length of this side.

The two shorter horizontal sides equal the length of the longer side opposite. So the missing side is 21 cm – 5 cm = 16 cm. Now add the sides together to find the perimeter: 21 + 6 + 16 + 6 + 5 + 12 = 66 cm.

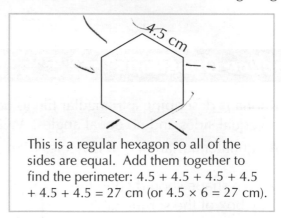

This is a regular hexagon so all of the sides are equal. Add them together to find the perimeter: 4.5 + 4.5 + 4.5 + 4.5 + 4.5 + 4.5 = 27 cm (or 4.5 × 6 = 27 cm).

Area *is the* **Space Inside** *a* **Shape**

Finding the **Area** of a **Square** or **Rectangle**

Multiply the <u>length</u> by the <u>width</u> to work out the area of a square or rectangle.

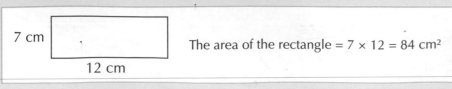

The area of the rectangle = 7 × 12 = 84 cm²

Area is measured in square units, e.g. cm² and m².

Finding the **Area** of a **Triangle**

Calculate the area of a triangle by <u>multiplying</u> half of the <u>base length</u> by the <u>height</u>.

You might see this as the formula: $area = \frac{1}{2} \times base \times height$

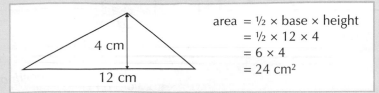

$$area = \frac{1}{2} \times base \times height$$
$$= \frac{1}{2} \times 12 \times 4$$
$$= 6 \times 4$$
$$= 24 \text{ cm}^2$$

Finding the **Area** of **Other Shapes**

Sometimes you need to <u>split</u> a more complex shape into <u>smaller shapes</u> to calculate its area.

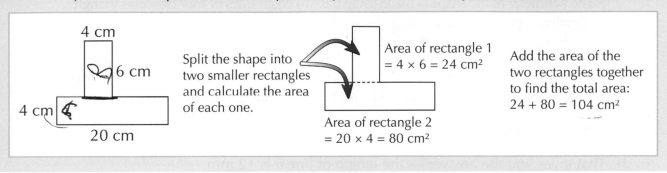

Split the shape into two smaller rectangles and calculate the area of each one.

Area of rectangle 1
$= 4 \times 6 = 24 \text{ cm}^2$

Area of rectangle 2
$= 20 \times 4 = 80 \text{ cm}^2$

Add the area of the two rectangles together to find the total area:
$24 + 80 = 104 \text{ cm}^2$

11+ *Style* Questions

Q Yasmin used 5 identical rectangular tiles to make the shape shown. The length of each tile is 16 cm and the width of each tile is 8 cm.

What is the perimeter of the arrow shape that's been made inside the grey tiles?

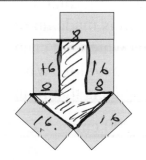

Method

1) Work out the <u>length</u> of each part of the shape.

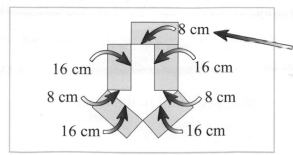

This side is the length of the top rectangle minus the width of the rectangle under it. $16 - 8 = 8$ cm.

2) <u>Add</u> each side together to find the perimeter.

$8 + 16 + 8 + 16 + 16 + 8 + 16 = 88$ cm

Q Marcelo made this shape using one square
and four identical isosceles triangles.
The total perimeter of the shape is 96 mm.
What is the length of line *a*?

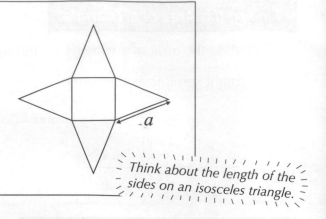

Think about the length of the sides on an isosceles triangle.

Method

1) Look at the <u>lines</u> which make up the <u>perimeter</u> of Marcelo's shape.

> The perimeter of the shape is made using the two equal sides of four isosceles triangles.
> There are eight lines that make up the perimeter of the shape.
> The isosceles triangles are identical, so all eight lines must be the same length.

2) You know that the perimeter of the shape is 96 mm. So, <u>divide</u> the total perimeter by the number of lines to work out the length of <u>each line</u>.

> $96 \div 8 = 12$ mm

3) That gives you the answer — the length of line *a* is <u>12 mm</u>.

Q Mabel is building a new run for her rabbits.
The run is made up of four rectangular fence
panels which are each 200 cm in length and
40 cm in width. What is the total area of the
fence panels that Mabel needs to make the run?

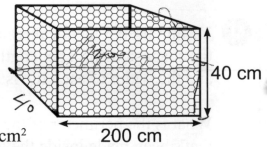

A 32 000 cm²   **C** 40 000 cm²   **E** 16 000 cm²

B 8000 cm²   **D** 24 000 cm²

Method

1) Start by finding the area of <u>each rectangular panel</u>.

> The area of a rectangle = length × width
> So the area of each fence panel = 200 × 40 = 8000 cm²

You can easily do 200 × 40 — take off the three zeros and do 2 × 4 = 8, then add the three zeros back onto the answer — 8000.

2) <u>Multiply</u> this by the <u>number of panels</u> to find the <u>total area</u> of all of the fence panels.

> $8000 \times 4 = 32\,000$ cm²

3) The total area of the fence panels used by Mabel is <u>32 000 cm²</u>.
So the correct answer is <u>option A</u>.

Section Five — Shape and Space

Q The diagram shows the downstairs of Stephen's house. Stephen wants to lay a new carpet in his living room and his dining room. What is the area of carpet that Stephen needs?

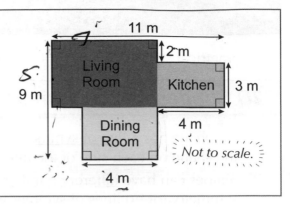

Not to scale.

A 35 m²   **C** 99 m²   **E** 51 m²

B 16 m²   **D** 63 m²

Method

1) You need to work out the areas of the living room and dining room <u>separately</u>, and then <u>add</u> them together.

2) Start by working out the <u>unknown lengths</u>.

The width of the living room is the width of the kitchen plus 2 metres.
3 + 2 = 5 m

The width of the dining room is the total width of the downstairs minus the width of the living room.
9 − 5 = 4 m

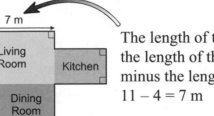

The length of the living room is the length of the whole downstairs minus the length of the kitchen.
11 − 4 = 7 m

3) Next, work out the area of the <u>living room</u> and the area of the <u>dining room</u>.

Area of the living room = 7 × 5 = 35 m²
Area of the dining room = 4 × 4 = 16 m²

4) <u>Add</u> the two areas together to find the <u>total area of carpet</u> that Stephen needs.

35 + 16 = 51 m² — option E is correct.

Practice Questions

1) This shape is made from two identical regular hexagons joined together. The total perimeter of the shape is 75 cm. How long is side Z?

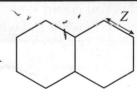

2) Calculate the area of this shape.

A 48 cm²   **C** 64 cm²   **E** 96 cm²
B 72 cm²   **D** 132 cm²

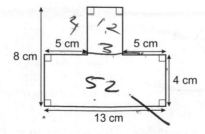

Section Five — Shape and Space

Symmetry

Symmetrical shapes can be split into two identical halves. These halves are reflections of each other.

2D Shapes can be Symmetrical

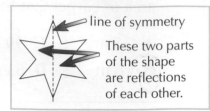

line of symmetry

These two parts of the shape are reflections of each other.

1) If a shape has a <u>line of symmetry</u>, it means that both parts of the shape on each side of the line are <u>reflections</u> of <u>each other</u>.

2) Shapes can have <u>different numbers</u> of lines of symmetry (or no lines of symmetry). For example:

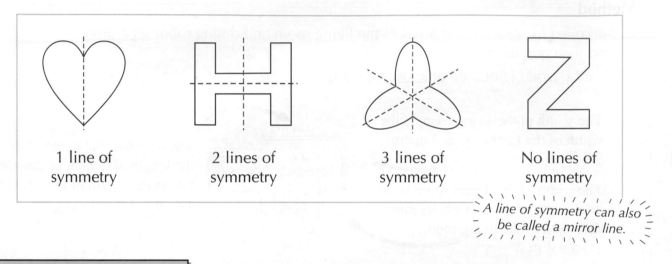

| 1 line of symmetry | 2 lines of symmetry | 3 lines of symmetry | No lines of symmetry |

A line of symmetry can also be called a mirror line.

11+ Style Questions

Q Charlene has drawn half of a shape. She reflects it in the mirror line to make a whole shape. What is the name of the whole shape?

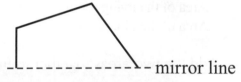 mirror line

A Rhombus **C** Pentagon **E** Kite

B Parallelogram **D** Hexagon

Method

1) You could sketch the shape and its <u>reflection</u> on some rough paper to show you what the <u>whole shape</u> will be.

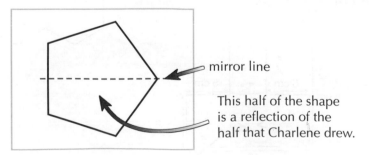

mirror line

This half of the shape is a reflection of the half that Charlene drew.

2) The whole shape has <u>five sides</u>. This means that it's a <u>pentagon</u> — option C.

Section Five — Shape and Space

Q How many lines of symmetry
does this shape have?

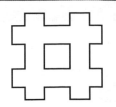

Method

1) Start by looking for any <u>horizontal</u> or <u>vertical lines of symmetry</u>.

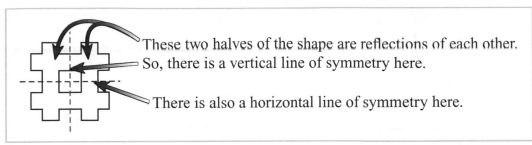

These two halves of the shape are reflections of each other.
So, there is a vertical line of symmetry here.

There is also a horizontal line of symmetry here.

2) Next, look for any <u>diagonal</u> lines of symmetry.

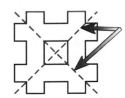

There are two diagonal lines of symmetry here.
The lines split the shape into two sets of identical halves.

3) The shape has <u>four lines of symmetry</u> in total.

Tips and Tricks for Symmetry

If you're stuck in the exam, you can draw the shape on a scrap piece of
paper and fold it in half. Unfold the paper again and look to see whether
the two halves of the shape on either side of the fold line are symmetrical.

Practice Questions

1) What whole shape would you see when this half shape
   is reflected in the mirror line?

   A Trapezium   **C** Rhombus   **E** Hexagon

   B Parallelogram   **D** Pentagon

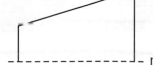

2) Elssie drew the following shape.
   How many lines of symmetry does it have?

Section Five — Shape and Space

3D Shapes

3D shapes are different from 2D shapes — they have a length, a width and a height.

Learn these common 3D Shapes

Cubes and Cuboids have Six Faces

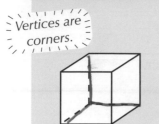

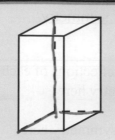

Vertices are corners.

Cube
6 faces, 12 edges
and 8 vertices

Cuboid
6 faces, 12 edges
and 8 vertices

Pyramids have Triangular Faces that join at a Point

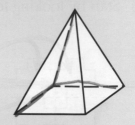

Triangle-based Pyramid
4 faces, 6 edges
and 4 vertices

Square-based Pyramid
5 faces, 8 edges
and 5 vertices

Prisms have the Same Face at Each End

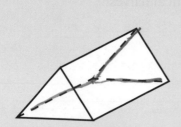

Triangular Prism
5 faces, 9 edges
and 6 vertices

Pentagonal Prism
7 faces, 15 edges
and 10 vertices

Hexagonal Prism
8 faces, 18 edges
and 12 vertices

Nets Fold to make 3D Shapes

1) 3D shapes can be made using a <u>net</u>. A net is a 2D shape which can be <u>folded</u> to make a 3D shape.

2) The shapes that make up the <u>net</u> become the faces of the <u>3D shape</u>.

3) There's often <u>more than one</u> net that you can use to make a 3D shape.

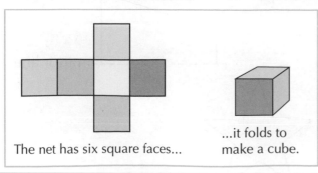

The net has six square faces...   ...it folds to make a cube.

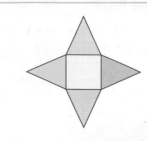

The net has four triangles around a square...   ...it folds to make a square-based pyramid.

Volume *of* Cubes *and* Cuboids = *Length × Width × Height*

1) <u>Volume</u> is the amount of space <u>inside</u> a shape.
2) You can work out the volume of a cube or a cuboid by <u>multiplying</u> the <u>length</u>, <u>width</u> and <u>height</u> together.

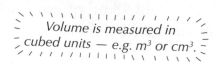

Volume is measured in cubed units — e.g. m^3 or cm^3.

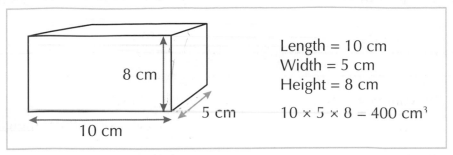

Length = 10 cm
Width = 5 cm
Height = 8 cm

$10 \times 5 \times 8 = 400 \ cm^3$

11+ *Style* Questions

Q Sunita has made the 3D shape shown on the right, and shaded part of two faces.
Which of the nets below will form Sunita's shape?

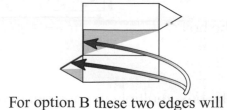

A   **B**   **C**   **D**   **E**

Method

1) <u>Imagine</u> each net being folded up.
   Work out which <u>edges of the shaded faces</u> will <u>join</u> together.

2) Work through the <u>options</u> until you find the <u>correct answer</u>:

The white half of the triangle must meet the grey half of the rectangle.

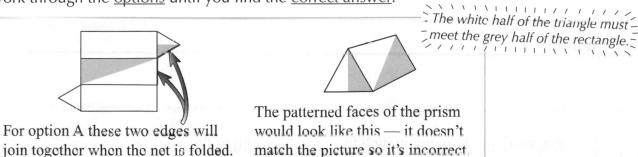

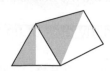

For option A these two edges will join together when the net is folded.

The patterned faces of the prism would look like this — it doesn't match the picture so it's incorrect.

For option B these two edges will join together when the net is folded.

The patterned faces of the prism would look like this — it matches the picture so option B is the correct answer.

3) You can <u>check</u> your answer by working through <u>options C-E</u>. <u>None</u> of them have the white half of the triangle meeting the shaded half of the rectangle, so they're all <u>incorrect</u>.

Q Chloe's swimming pool is shown.
It can hold 48 m³ of water when full.
What is the height of the swimming pool?

A 1.5 m   C 12 m   E 8 m

B 4 m   D 2 m

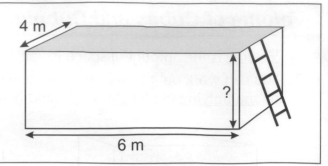

4 m

6 m

?

Method

1) The <u>formula</u> to work out the volume of the pool is: <u>length × width × height</u>.

2) You know the volume, the length and the width, so you can use this to work out the <u>height</u>.

> length × width × height = 48 m³
> 6 × 4 × height = 48 m³
> 24 × height = 48 m³
> Now work out how many 24s make 48. 24 × 2 = 48.

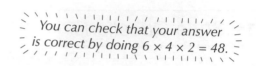
You can check that your answer is correct by doing 6 × 4 × 2 = 48.

3) The height of the swimming pool is <u>2 m</u> — <u>option D</u>.

Q Oscar has a bag of identical dice of side 2 cm.
What is the maximum number of dice that he can fit in this box?

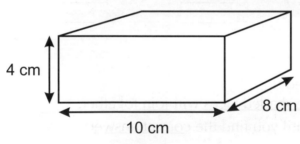

4 cm

10 cm

8 cm

Method

1) Start by working out <u>how many dice</u> fit along the <u>length</u> of the box.

> Each dice is 2 cm long and the box is 10 cm long. 10 ÷ 2 = 5 dice.

2) Next, work out <u>how many dice</u> fit along the <u>width</u> of the box.

> Each dice is 2 cm wide and the box is 8 cm wide. 8 ÷ 2 = 4 dice.

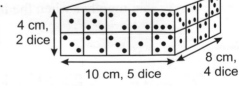
4 cm, 2 dice

10 cm, 5 dice

8 cm, 4 dice

3) Then, work out <u>how many dice</u> fit up the <u>height</u> of the box.

> Each dice is 2 cm high and the box is 4 cm high. 4 ÷ 2 = 2 dice.

4) To work out the <u>total number</u> of dice that will fit in the box, <u>multiply</u> the number of dice that fit in the <u>length</u>, by the number that fit in the <u>width</u>, and the number that fit up the <u>height</u>.

> 5 × 4 × 2 = 40. Oscar will be able to fit 40 dice in the box.

Section Five — Shape and Space

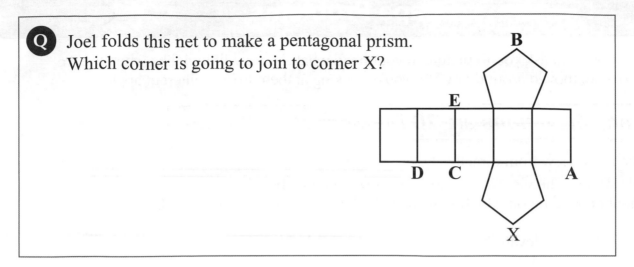

Q Joel folds this net to make a pentagonal prism.
Which corner is going to join to corner X?

Method

1) You need to imagine <u>how</u> the net will be folded to make the pentagonal prism.
2) Each corner of the <u>two pentagons</u> will join with a corner of a <u>rectangle</u>.

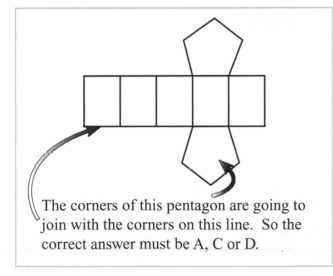

The corners of this pentagon are going to join with the corners on this line. So the correct answer must be A, C or D.

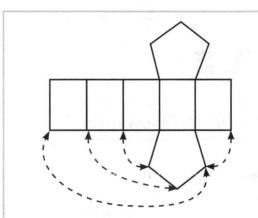

Corner X is going to join to corner D. So, the correct answer is option D.

Practice Questions

1) Which of these nets will not fold to make a cube?

   A   B   C   D   E

2) Vegetable stock cubes have sides that are 1 cm long. How many vegetable stock cubes will fit in a box that is 4 cm long, 8 cm wide and 2 cm high?

3) Frankie has made this net.
   What shape will be made when the net is folded?

Section Five — Shape and Space

Shape Problems

Some questions will ask you to picture in your head what shapes will look like when they're flipped, rotated, moved around or when you're looking at them from a different angle.

Plans and Elevations are 2D Drawings of 3D Shapes

1) A <u>plan</u> is the view from directly <u>above</u> a shape.

2) An <u>elevation</u> is the view from <u>one side</u>. Elevations can be different depending on which side you're looking at.

Elevations are also called projections.

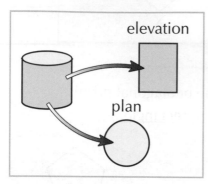

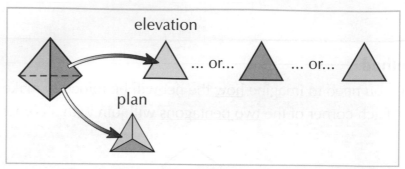

11+ Style Questions

Q Some triangular tiles have been used to make a pattern. The tiles are reflected in a vertical mirror line to the right-hand side, then rotated 90° clockwise. Which of the options shows the shape now?

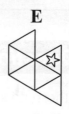

    A   **B**   **C**   **D**   **E**

 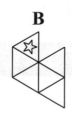 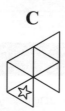  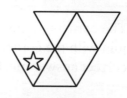

── **Method** ──────────────

1) Imagine the tiles being reflected in a vertical mirror line, then rotated 90° clockwise.

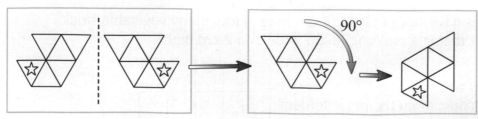

2) <u>Option C</u> is the correct answer.

Q Here is a 3D shape built out of cubes.
Which of the following plans matches
the shape?

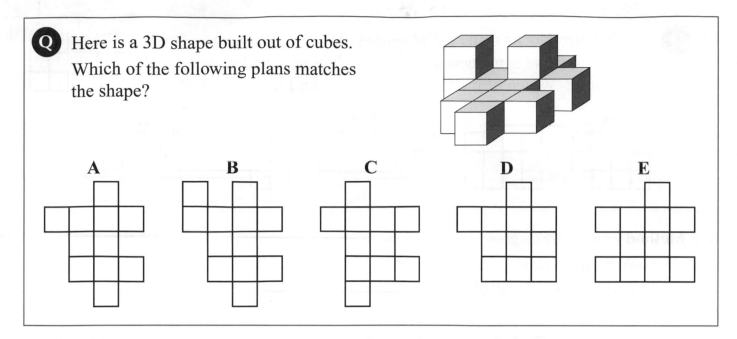

A   B   C   D   E

Method

1) You can <u>ignore</u> the cubes on the bottom of other cubes — you <u>wouldn't see them</u> from above.

2) It can be helpful to choose a part of the shape and use it as a <u>point of reference</u>.

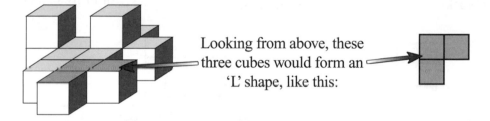

Looking from above, these
three cubes would form an
'L' shape, like this:

3) <u>All</u> the options have a part that looks like this, so
add on a <u>bit more</u> to your point of reference.

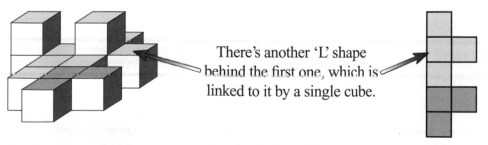

There's another 'L' shape
behind the first one, which is
linked to it by a single cube.

4) Options <u>A</u> and <u>B</u> have a part that looks like this.

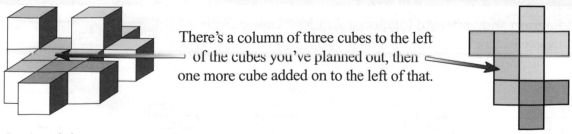

There's a column of three cubes to the left
of the cubes you've planned out, then
one more cube added on to the left of that.

5) <u>Option A</u> is correct.

Section Five — Shape and Space

Q Lily has two blocks made out of square tiles. She fits them together to make some new shapes. She does not overlap the two blocks. Which of the following shapes can Lily not make?

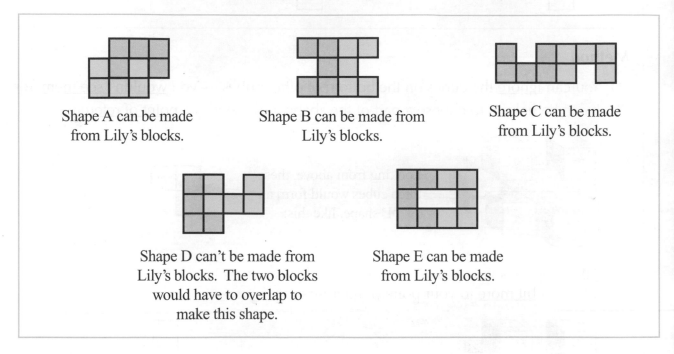

A   **B**   **C**   **D**   **E**

Method

1) Look at <u>each</u> answer option and see if it can be made from Lily's blocks.

2) You need to imagine <u>rotating the blocks</u> to see if they can make the shapes.

Shape A can be made from Lily's blocks.

Shape B can be made from Lily's blocks.

Shape C can be made from Lily's blocks.

Shape D can't be made from Lily's blocks. The two blocks would have to overlap to make this shape.

Shape E can be made from Lily's blocks.

3) <u>Option D</u> is the correct answer — it can't be made from Lily's blocks.

Practice Question

1) The diagram shows how a logo on a window appears when viewed from the front. Which of the following options shows the same logo when viewed from the back?

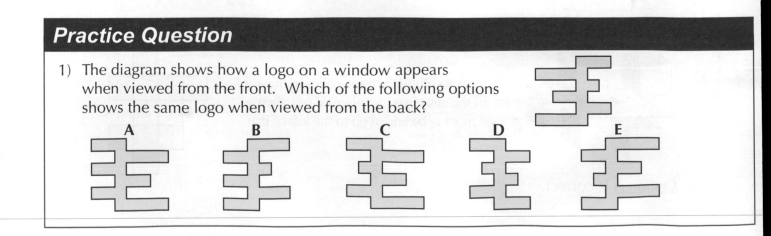

A   **B**   **C**   **D**   **E**

Coordinates

Coordinates are pairs of numbers that help you to find points on a grid.

Coordinates show a Point on a Grid

1) Each point on a grid has <u>two numbers</u> to show its position. These are <u>coordinates</u>.
2) The first number shows the position on the <u>horizontal x-axis</u>.
   The second number shows the position on the <u>vertical y-axis</u>.
3) Coordinates are always written <u>in brackets</u>, for example (0, 0) or (5, 4).

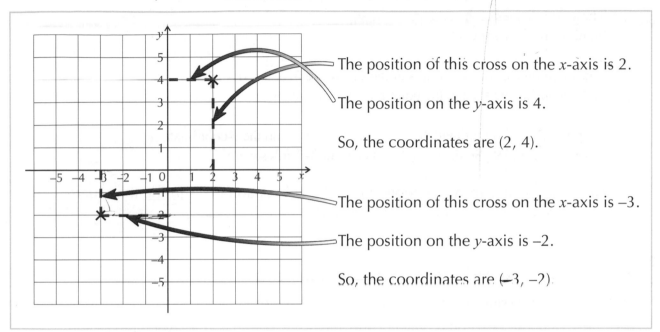

The position of this cross on the x-axis is 2.

The position on the y-axis is 4.

So, the coordinates are (2, 4).

The position of this cross on the x-axis is –3.

The position on the y-axis is –2.

So, the coordinates are (–3, –2).

11+ Style Questions

Q A rectangle was drawn on a coordinate grid. What are the coordinates of corner A?

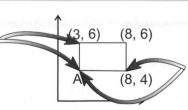

Method

1) You can use the coordinates you've been given to work out the coordinates of <u>corner A</u>.

These two corners are on the same position on the x-axis. The x-axis coordinate of the top corner is 3, so the x-axis coordinate of A is also 3.

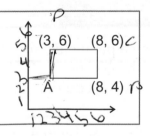

These two corners are on the same position on the y-axis. The y-axis coordinate of the right-hand corner is 4, so the y-axis coordinate of A is also 4.

2) That gives you the <u>x-axis</u> and <u>y-axis</u> coordinates. So, the coordinates of corner A are (<u>3, 4</u>).

handwritten: x = 3   y = 5
x = 7   y = 9

Q Yohan draws a square on a grid. The coordinates of the four corners are (3, 5), (7, 5), (3, 9) and (7, 9). Which of the following points is inside Yohan's square?

   A (7, 3)   **B** (6, 4)   **C** (9, 8)   **D** (6, 8)   **E** (5, 4)

Method

1) You can use the <u>coordinates</u> that you've been <u>given</u> to work out which of the coordinates is <u>within</u> the square.

> The *x*-coordinates of the corners of the square are 3, 7, 3 and 7.
> So to be inside the square, the point must have an *x*-coordinate between 3 and 7.

> The *y*-coordinates of the corners of the square are 5, 5, 9 and 9.
> So to be inside the square, the point must have a *y*-coordinate between 5 and 9.

> In option D, the *x*-coordinate (6) is between 3 and 7, and the *y*-coordinate (8) is between 5 and 9. So the point (6, 8) is inside Yohan's square.

2) That gives you the answer — <u>option D</u> is the only option that's <u>inside</u> the square.

Tips and Tricks for Coordinates Problems

If you're stuck with a question like this in the exam and you have a rough piece of paper, you could sketch a grid and use it to help you answer the question.

Practice Questions

1) Nadine is plotting a parallelogram on this coordinate grid.
   She plots two of the corners at (1, 3) and (2, 6).
   Which of the following could be the coordinates of the other two corners?
   A (4, 3) and (5, 4)   **C** (6, 5) and (6, 4)   **E** (3, 2) and (4, 7)
   B (5, 5) and (7, 7)   **D** (7, 6) and (6, 3)

2) The farmhouse is exactly halfway between the campsite and car park.
   What are the coordinates of the farmhouse?

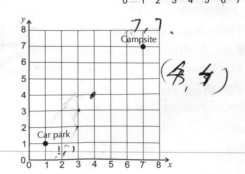

Section Five — Shape and Space

Transformations

Transformations are where shapes are reflected or moved around a coordinate grid.

Shapes can be Transformed on a Coordinate Grid

The shape you get when a shape has been transformed is sometimes called its image.

Reflection in a Line

1) Shapes can be <u>reflected</u> across a <u>mirror line</u> on a coordinate grid.
2) Each point and its reflection are exactly the <u>same distance</u> from the mirror line.

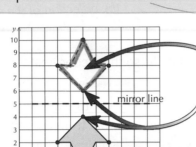

This is the reflection of the shape.

This point on the original shape is one square away from the mirror line. So, the same point on the reflected shape is also one square away from the mirror line.

Translation is Sliding a Shape

<u>Translation</u> is when a shape is <u>moved</u> from one place to another, without being flipped or rotated.

This shape has been translated by moving it 5 squares right and 4 squares down:

When you translate a shape, the new shape should look exactly the same as the original.

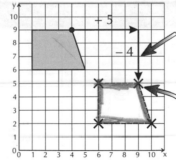

For the red point (4, 9), the *x*-coordinate on the translated shape will be 5 greater, and the *y*-coordinate will be 4 fewer.

The *x*-coordinate of this corner will be $4 + 5 = 9$ and the *y*-coordinate will be $9 - 4 = 5$ — (9, 5).

11+ Style Questions

> **Q** Point P (5, 2) is one vertex of a shape.
> The shape is translated 4 squares to the left and 2 squares up.
> What are the coordinates of the translated point P?

Method

The *x*-coordinate of point P <u>decreases</u> by 4 and the *y*-coordinate <u>increases</u> by 2.

The coordinates of the translated point P are $(5 - 4, 2 + 2) = (1, 4)$

(5, 10) 5

Q Gurbaj drew this shape on a coordinate grid.
She then reflected the shape in the mirror line.
What are the coordinates of the image of point X?

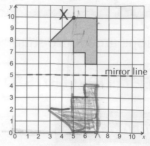

(15, 10)

Method

Point X on the <u>image</u> will be the <u>same distance</u>
from the mirror line as point X is on the original shape.

If you're allowed to write on the exam paper, you could draw the reflection of the shape.

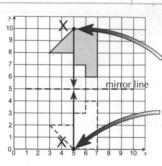

The shape has been reflected vertically, so the x-coordinate is still the same (5).

The y-coordinate of point X is 10, and the y-coordinate of the mirror line is 5. So, point X is $10 - 5 = 5$ squares away from the mirror line.

The image of point X will also be 5 squares away from the mirror line. So, its y-coordinate will be $5 - 5 = 0$.

The coordinates of the image of point X are (5, 0).

Practice Questions

1) What will the coordinates of corner Y
be after this triangle has been
reflected in the mirror line?

(6, 4)

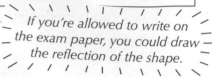

2) The shape on the coordinate grid
is translated 6 squares to the left
and 3 squares down.
What are the new coordinates of point Z?

(−1, 4)

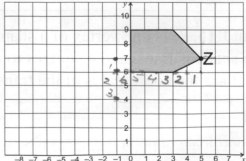

Units

For the exam, you'll need to be able to convert between different size units of measurement, as well as have an idea of how big each one is.

Warm-Up Activity

Have a look at some tins, packets and bottles from your kitchen cupboards. Try to guess the <u>mass</u> or <u>volume</u> of each. Check the labels to see how close you were.

There are Units for **Length**, **Mass** and **Volume**

1) Here's a bit about the different <u>units of length</u>:

A flea is about 2 mm long.

Your finger is about 1 cm wide.

A door is about 2 m tall.

1 centimetre = 10 millimetres
1 metre = 100 centimetres
1 kilometre = 1000 metres

10 football pitches laid end-to-end would be about 1 km.

2) Here's a bit about the different <u>units of mass</u>:

A paper clip has a mass of about 1 g.

A medium-sized bag of sugar has a mass of 1 kg.

1 kilogram = 1000 grams

'Capacity' is the volume that something can hold when it's full, e.g. the capacity of a large carton of juice might be 1 litre.

3) Here's a bit about the different <u>units of volume</u>:

A bottle of squash often holds 1 litre.

1 litre = 1000 millilitres

A small drop of water is about 1 ml.

Some **Scales** are **Tricky** to **Read**

1) Units of measurement are often displayed using <u>scales</u>.

2) You need to be able to <u>read</u> values off scales, but not all divisions on scales are marked with a <u>number</u>. Here's an example:

What value (in litres) is the arrow pointing to?

To work out what value the arrow is pointing to, you need to work out what each division is worth.

There are 5 divisions between the numbered marks.

The difference between the numbered marks is 0.1 litres.

So each division shows 0.1 litres ÷ 5 = 0.02 litres.

The arrow is pointing to 1.46 litres.

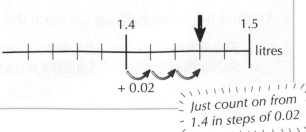

+ 0.02

Just count on from 1.4 in steps of 0.02

Convert between **Large** and **Small** Units by **Multiplying** or **Dividing**

1) You might need to <u>convert</u> a <u>smaller</u> unit into a <u>larger</u> unit or a <u>larger</u> unit into a <u>smaller</u> one.

2) To convert a larger unit to a smaller unit you need to <u>multiply</u>. For example:

> To convert a mass that's in kg to a mass that's in g,
> multiply by 1000 (because there are 1000 g in a kg).
> $$3.6 \text{ kg} \implies 3.6 \times 1000 = 3600 \text{ g}$$

3) To convert a smaller unit to a larger unit you need to <u>divide</u>. For example:

> To convert a length that's in cm to a length that's in m,
> divide by 100 (because there are 100 cm in a m).
> $$40 \text{ cm} \implies 40 \div 100 = 0.4 \text{ m}$$

11+ **Style** Questions

> **Q** How much water is there in this measuring jug?
>
>   A   0.95 litres
>   B   0.8 litres
>   C   0.75 litres
>   D   0.85 litres
>   E   0.9 litres

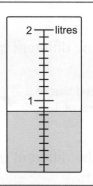

Method

1) Work out how much each <u>division</u> on the scale is <u>worth</u>.

> There are 10 divisions between the numbered marks, and the difference
> between the numbered marks is 1 litre. So each division shows:
> $1 \div 10 = 0.1$ litres

2) The level of water in the jug is <u>halfway</u> between two marks on the scale.
    Work out the <u>value</u> of those two marks.

> Each division shows 0.1 litres. The water is between the eighth
> and ninth division, so there is between 0.8 and 0.9 litres.

3) Find the value <u>halfway</u> between the two marks.

> The difference between 0.8 and 0.9 is 0.1. Half of 0.1 is 0.05.
> So, halfway between 0.8 and 0.9 is 0.85, so the answer is D.

Q Jo has 1.6 kg of hot chocolate powder. She puts 30 g of powder in each of 5 mugs of hot water. How much hot chocolate powder does Jo have left?

A 1.57 kg   B 1.3 kg   C 1.45 kg   D 0.1 kg   E 1.585 kg

Method

1) First work out how many grams of hot chocolate powder have been <u>used</u>.

> 30 g in each of 5 mugs is a total of $30 \times 5 = 150$ g.

2) To find out how much hot chocolate powder is left you need to <u>subtract 150 g from 1.6 kg</u>, so make the <u>units</u> the same. The answers are in <u>kg</u>, so make the units <u>both kg</u>.

> $150 \text{ g} \div 1000 = 0.15$ kg

3) Now <u>subtract</u> to find the mass of hot chocolate powder left.

> $1.6 \text{ kg} - 0.15 \text{ kg} = 1.45$ kg. So the answer is C.

Q A stalactite is hanging from a cave ceiling. It is currently 22 cm long. If it grows at a rate of 0.2 mm per year, how long, in centimetres, will it be in 200 years' time?

Method

1) First, find out how much the stalactite will <u>grow in 200 years</u> by multiplying 0.2 mm by 200.

> The quick way to do 0.2×200 is to work out 0.2×100, and multiply the result by 2:
> $0.2 \times 100 = 20$
> $20 \times 2 = 40$ mm

2) You need to add the new growth to the stalactite's <u>current length</u> — but first make sure the <u>units</u> are the <u>same</u>.

> As you want the final answer in cm, convert the new growth to cm.
> 1 cm = 10 mm, so divide 40 mm by 10 to get the number of cm: $40 \div 10 = 4$ cm

3) Now <u>add</u> the current length and the new growth to find the length in 200 years' time.

> Length of stalactite = 22 cm + 4 cm = 26 cm

Practice Questions

1) Which of the following is most likely to be the mass of Tim's schoolbag with all of his books in?
   A 0.3 g   B 3 g   C 30 g   D 3 kg   E 30 kg

2) There are 28.75 litres of soup. 350 ml is spilt, and the rest is divided into 400 ml servings. How many servings are there?

3) Ben's stride is 50 cm. How many strides must he take to walk 10 km?
   A 20 000   B 2000   C 200 000   D 500   E 5000

Section Six — Units and Measures

Time

There's a lot to remember for this topic. Time to get prepared...

There are lots of **Different Units** for **Measuring Time**

1) Here's how some of the different <u>units of time</u> are <u>related</u> to each other. ➡

   1 minute = 60 seconds
   1 hour = 60 minutes
   1 day = 24 hours
   1 year = 365 days (366 in a leap year)

   Leap years occur every 4 years. The extra day is added to February.

2) There are <u>7 days</u> in a week and <u>52 weeks</u> in a <u>year</u>.

3) Months are a bit more tricky — there are <u>12 months</u> in a year, but the number of days in each month is <u>different</u>.

4) You can memorise the number of <u>days</u> in <u>each month</u> using this poem. ➡

   "30 days has September, April, June and November.
   All the rest have 31, except February alone,
   Which has 28 days clear, and 29 in each leap year."

Don't Get Confused between **Morning** and **Evening**

1) The <u>hours</u> on a <u>12-hour clock</u> are shown by the numbers <u>1-12</u>. The numbers then have either "<u>am</u>" or "<u>pm</u>" after them to show you whether it's <u>morning</u> or <u>evening</u>.

2) "<u>am</u>" runs from 12 midnight to 11:59 in the morning.

3) "<u>pm</u>" runs from 12 noon to 11:59 at night.

4) 24-hour time is the <u>same</u> as 12-hour time if it's <u>morning</u>, e.g. 9:00 am is the same as 09:00 on a 24-hour clock.

5) But you have to <u>add on 12 hours</u> if it's <u>afternoon</u> or <u>evening</u>, e.g. 1:00 pm is the same as 13:00 on a 24-hour clock.

6) When it gets to <u>midnight</u>, the 24-hour clock goes from 23:59 to <u>00:00</u>.

24-hour times always have 4 digits. A "0" is added to the front if it's before 10:00.

11+ Style Questions

> **Q** Which of the following 24-hour times is the same as ten to three in the afternoon?
> A 15:10   B 02:.   C 15:50   D 14:50   E 03:50

Method

1) "Ten to three" in the afternoon in 12-hour time is <u>2:50 pm</u>.

2) Because it's in the <u>afternoon</u>, you add 12 hours to convert it to the 24-hour clock.

   2:50 + 12 hours = 14:50. So the answer is D.

Q John spent 45 minutes weeding and then 52 minutes mowing the grass. How long did he spend gardening?

A 1.37 hours   **B** 1 hour 37 minutes   C 137 hours   D 9.7 hours   E 97 hours

Method

1) Add the number of minutes together to get the <u>total</u>. ➡ | 45 + 52 = 97 minutes |

2) Convert this to <u>hours and minutes</u>.

> There are 60 minutes in one hour. If you subtract 60 from 97 you're left with 37 minutes (97 − 60 = 37). So 97 minutes = 1 hour and 37 minutes — the answer is B.

1.37 hours is not the same as 1 hour 37 minutes because there are 60 minutes in 1 hour and not 100.

 Q Jane was born on Saturday 8th March. What day of the week was Ben born on if he was born on 4th May the same year?

Method

1) First, find <u>how many days</u> there are <u>between</u> the two dates. You can do this in short, easy stages — write down the numbers of days in <u>each month</u> between the dates.

> 8th March   31 − 8 = <u>23</u> days   31st March   <u>30</u> days   30th April   <u>4</u> days   4th May
>
> Now add up the number of days: 23 + 30 + 4 = 57 days

2) There are 7 days in a week, so every <u>7th</u> day after 8th March will be a Saturday too. Find the <u>multiple of 7</u> which is closest to 57.

> 8 × 7 = 56. So the 56th day after 8th March is a Saturday.

3) Now work out the <u>day</u> that 4th May falls on.

> There are 57 days between 8th March and 4th May, and the 56th day is a Saturday. So 4th May must be a Sunday.

Tips and Tricks for Time Questions

The method used to find the difference between two dates can be used to find the difference between two times. E.g. to find the number of minutes between 9:46 am and 11:31 am:

> 9:46   14 mins   10:00   60 mins   11:00   31 mins   11:31
>
> 14 + 60 + 31 = 105 minutes

Section Six — Units and Measures

Q Hannah needs to get to Millham by 2 pm. What is the latest that she can get a bus from Dale Street?

Ulverstown	1254	1314	1334	1404
Dale Street	1259	1319	1339	1409
Railway Station	1308	1327	1348	1417
Canal Foot		1340		1430
Millham	1324	1347	1404	1437
Daltown	1345	1411	1425	1511

Times in timetables are often written without a colon, so 1254 is the same as 12:54.

Method

1) Hannah needs to get to Millham by <u>2 pm</u>, but the timetable is in <u>24-hour clock time</u>. Convert 2 pm to the 24-hour clock.

> It's in the afternoon, so add 12 hours: 2 pm = 2 + 12 = 14:00

2) Now find the row for <u>Millham</u>. This lists the times that buses arrive there.

3) Find the <u>latest time</u> before 14:00 that Hannah can arrive at Millham.

> The bus that arrives at 14:04 is too late. The one before gets in at 13:47.

Ulverstown	1254	1314	1334	1404
Dale Street	1259	1319	1339	1409
Railway Station	1308	1327	1348	1417
Canal Foot		1340		1430
Millham	1324	1347	1404	1437
Daltown	1345	1411	1425	1511

4) Look <u>up the column</u> to find when this bus leaves Dale Street.

> It leaves Dale Street at 13:19.

Practice Questions

1) Some children's birthdays are given below. Which child is youngest?

Meg — 14th May 2009   Fred — 16th March 2009   Geeta — 1st February 2008
Jim — 28th December 2008   Max — 13th October 2009

2) Kerry completes one page of her maths book each day, starting on 1st September. If there are 154 pages, in which month will she finish her book?

3) Jamie starts his homework at 4:53 pm. If he finishes it at 7:15 pm, how long did it take?

A 2.22 hours   **C** 22 hours 2 minutes   **E** 3 hours 38 minutes
B 202 minutes   **D** 2 hours 22 minutes

Section Six — Units and Measures

Mixed Problems

Some questions test your knowledge of more than one topic, so you might have to read a pie chart and work out some angles. The questions on these pages are examples, but you could be tested on any different combination of topics.

Warm-Up Activity

Draw a <u>line</u> between the calculations which have the <u>same answer</u>.

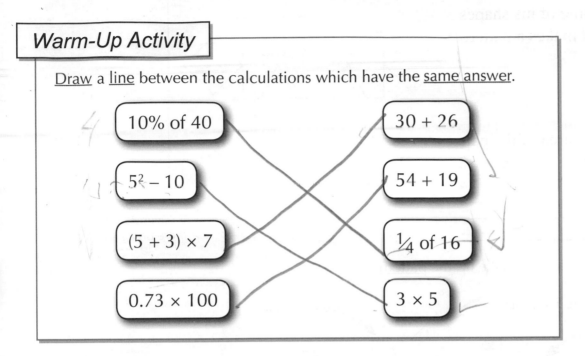

10% of 40	30 + 26
$5^2 - 10$	54 + 19
(5 + 3) × 7	¼ of 16
0.73 × 100	3 × 5

11+ Style Questions

Q A cruise ship travels 30½ kilometres every hour.
It left port at 7 pm on Monday and arrived at its destination at 1 am on Tuesday.

How far did it travel?   _____

Method

1) Work out how many <u>hours</u> the cruise ship was <u>travelling</u> for.

> On Monday the ship travelled for 5 hours between 7 pm and 12 midnight.
> On Tuesday the ship travelled for 1 hour between 12 midnight and 1 am.
> 5 + 1 = 6 hours.

2) Now multiply <u>6 hours</u> by <u>30½ kilometres</u>.

> Use partitioning to find 6 × 30½. Partition 30½ into 30 and ½.
> 6 × 30 = 180, and 6 × ½ = 3 (it's the same as half of 6).
> Add together your results, 180 + 3 = 183 km.

3) The ship travelled <u>183 kilometres</u>.

Q Dylan has some shapes which have areas q and r.

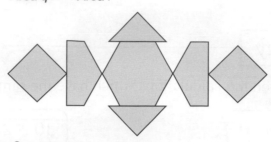

Area q Area r

He cuts some of his shapes in half and makes a pattern.

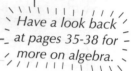

What is the area of the pattern?

A $2q + 3r$ C $3q + 2r$ E $4q + 4r$

B $3q + r$ D $3q + 4r$

Have a look back at pages 35-38 for more on algebra.

Method

1) Work out what shapes make up the <u>pattern</u>.

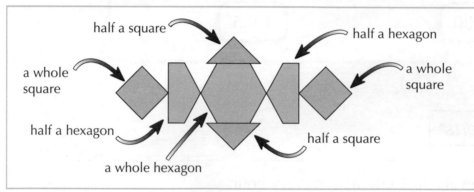

half a square   half a hexagon

a whole square   a whole square

half a hexagon   half a square

a whole hexagon

2) Now <u>add together</u> all of the <u>areas</u>.

There are two whole squares and two half squares: $2 + \frac{1}{2} + \frac{1}{2} = 3$
The pattern has a total of 3 squares, each with area q, so they have an area of $3q$.

There is one whole hexagon and two half hexagons: $1 + \frac{1}{2} + \frac{1}{2} = 2$
The pattern has a total of 2 hexagons, each with area r, so they have an area of $2r$.

The total area of the pattern is the areas of the shapes added together, $3q + 2r$.

3) So the <u>answer</u> is <u>C</u>.

Tips and Tricks for Mixed Problems

Make sure you read mixed problem questions very carefully.

They can look quite difficult, but you just need to make sure you

work out what steps you need to follow to find the answer.

Q Cliff wants to varnish all four walls of his barn.

Two of the walls of the barn are 15 metres long and 2.5 metres high. The other two walls are 9 metres long and 2.5 metres high.

1 litre of varnish will cover 10 square metres.

How many litres of varnish does he need?

Method

1) Work out the <u>total area</u> of all of the <u>walls</u>.

> The area of a rectangle = length × height.
> The lengths of all the walls would be 15 + 15 + 9 + 9 = 48 m.
> So the area of all the walls = 48 m × 2.5 m.
>
> Use partitioning to find 48 × 2.5. Partition 2.5 into 2 and 0.5.
> 48 × 2 = 96, and 48 × 0.5 = 24 (it's the same as half of 48).
> Add together your results, 96 + 24 = 120 m².

You could also work out the area of each wall and add them together.

2) Work out how many <u>litres</u> of <u>varnish</u> are needed to <u>cover</u> the <u>four walls</u>.

> 1 litre of varnish will cover 10 m². So 120 ÷ 10 = 12.
> 12 litres of varnish will cover the walls of the barn.

Q Calculate the size of angle x.

  A 25°   D 15°
  B 40°   E 10°
  C 30°

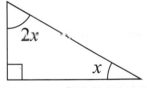

Method

1) Use the information you have to make an <u>equation</u>.

> Angles in a triangle add up to 180°.
> One of the angles is a right angle (90°) so the other
> two angles must add up to 180° − 90° = 90°.
> $2x + x = 90°$
> So $3x = 90°$.

2) Use your <u>equation</u> to find the size of <u>angle x</u>.

> Find x when $3x = 90°$.
>
> $3x = 90°$ The opposite of × 3 is ÷ 3,
> $3x ÷ 3 = 90° ÷ 3$ so divide both sides by 3.
>
> $x = 30°$ That gives you the answer — x is 30°.
>   C is correct.

Q Jason's class conducted a survey. They asked the teachers who drove to school how many passengers they took with them.

They collected their results in a bar chart.

What percentage of the teachers travelled with 3 passengers?

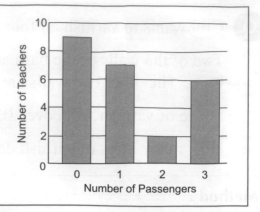

Method

1) First work out <u>how many teachers</u> took part in the <u>survey</u>.

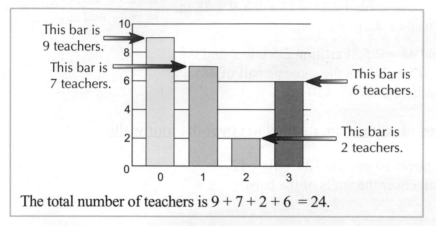

This bar is 9 teachers.
This bar is 7 teachers.
This bar is 6 teachers.
This bar is 2 teachers.

The total number of teachers is $9 + 7 + 2 + 6 = 24$.

2) Now you can work out the <u>percentage</u> of <u>teachers</u> who travelled with <u>3 passengers</u>.

6 teachers out of a total of 24 travelled with three passengers. This gives you the fraction $^6/_{24}$. This fraction can be simplified to $^1/_4$.

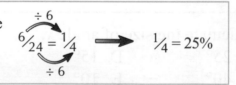

$^6/_{24} = ^1/_4 \longrightarrow ^1/_4 = 25\%$

3) The <u>percentage</u> of <u>teachers</u> who travelled with <u>3 passengers</u> is <u>25%</u>.

Practice Questions

1) A swimming pool is 10 metres long, 10 metres wide and 1.6 metres deep.
It costs 25p to fill 1 m³ of the pool with water.
What is the cost of filling the pool to the top?

2) Mr O'Brian recorded the colour of the flowers in his garden in a pie chart. What percentage of his flowers were red?

   A 5%
   B 12.5%
   C 25%
   D 42%
   E 54%
   F 45%

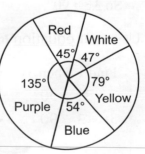

Glossary

acute angles	Angles that measure <u>less than</u> 90°. They are <u>smaller</u> than <u>right angles</u>.
area	The <u>amount of space</u> covered by a 2D (flat) shape. It is measured in <u>square units</u> (e.g. cm²).
average	A <u>typical</u> (or 'normal' value). The <u>mean</u> is a type of average.
coordinates	They tell you the <u>position</u> of a point on a grid. For example, (3, 4) means 3 units along the <u>horizontal *x*-axis</u> and 4 units up the <u>vertical *y*-axis</u>.
decimal places	The <u>places in a number</u> to the <u>right</u> of the decimal point. For example, the number 4.56 has 2 decimal places.
degrees, °	The units used to measure <u>angles</u>. For example, a right angle measures 90°.
denominator	The <u>bottom number</u> of a fraction.
equivalent	Something that has the same value. For example, ½ and ²/₄ are <u>equivalent fractions</u>.
estimate	An estimate is a <u>sensible guess</u> at the answer. You can use <u>rounding</u> to help you estimate answers.
factor	A whole number that divides exactly into another whole number. For example, the factors of 6 are 1, 2, 3 and 6.
frequency	<u>How many times</u> something appears in a set of data.
mass	Mass is what most people mean when they say 'weight'. A <u>brick</u> has a greater mass than a loaf of <u>bread</u>. Mass is measured in grams or kilograms.
multiple	Multiples are the <u>numbers</u> in a <u>times table</u> that goes on forever. For example, the multiples of 4 are 4, 8, 12, 16....
numerator	The <u>top number</u> of a fraction.
obtuse angles	Angles that measure <u>more than</u> 90° but less than 180°. They're <u>bigger</u> than <u>right angles</u>.
parallel	Parallel lines, faces and edges are always the <u>same distance apart</u>. They will <u>never meet</u> or cross.
perimeter	The distance around the <u>outside</u> of a shape.
perpendicular	Lines, faces or edges that meet each other at <u>right angles</u> (or would meet at right angles if you extended them) are perpendicular.
polygon	A <u>2D</u> (flat) shape with <u>straight sides</u>.
prime	A <u>prime number</u> is a number that has exactly <u>two</u> factors: <u>1 and itself</u>. For example, 2, 3, 5 and 7 are all prime numbers.
prime factor	A <u>factor</u> of a larger number which is also a <u>prime number</u>. Any whole number that isn't prime can be split up into a set of prime factors. For example, 5 and 2 are the prime factors of 10.
ratio	A comparison between one part and <u>another part</u>. For example, if there were 4 girls and 1 boy on a bus, the ratio of boys to girls would be 1 : 4.
square number	The result of <u>multiplying</u> a number by <u>itself</u>. For example, 3 × 3 = 9 is a square number.

Answers

SECTION ONE — WORKING WITH NUMBERS

PAGES 4-5 — PLACE VALUE
Warm-Up Activity
10 000 — Biggest, 1 — Smallest

The numbers in order from smallest to biggest are 1, 10, 100, 1000, 10 000. 10 000 is the biggest and 1 is the smallest.

1.   E

All the numbers have the same units, 8, so you need to look at the tenths. 4 of the numbers have 4 in the tenths (Option B has 5, so it's not the answer), which means you need to look at the hundredths. Option E has the smallest number of hundredths, 3, so E is the answer.

2.   B

A — incorrect, the numbers are 0.03 and 0.3 away from 7.
B — correct, both numbers are 0.11 away from 7.
C — incorrect, the numbers are 0.2 and 0.02 away from 7.
D — incorrect, the numbers are 0.06 and 0.1 away from 7.
E — incorrect, the numbers are 0.1 and 0.19 away from 7.

PAGE 7 — ROUNDING UP AND DOWN

1.   D

In 174 782, the 7 (in the ten thousands column) is being rounded. The 4 (in the thousands column) is less than 5 so 174 782 rounds down to 170 000.

2.   129.5 km

First convert the number of kilometres into metres so it's easier to work with:
129.456 km × 1000 = 129 456 m
The digit you are rounding is in the 100s column — 4. The digit to the right of it is 5, which means that you need to round up:
129 456 m rounds up to 129 500 m
The question asks you to give your answer in kilometres, so convert the figure in metres to kilometres:
129 500 m ÷ 1000 = 129.5 km

PAGE 9 — ADDITION

1.   B

Round each value to the nearest whole pound.
£13.89 rounds up to £14.00.
£3.35 rounds down to £3.00.
£12.30 rounds down to £12.00.
Add the rounded values together to estimate the answer:
£14.00 + £3.00 + 12.00 = £29.00.
The answer is either B or D. As you rounded down by 65p and up by 11p the estimate is lower than the actual answer. So the actual answer must be B — £29.54.
(You could also use a written method for this question.)

2.   48.43 seconds

Add the four numbers together using the column method:

```
  1 2 . 3 7
  1 1 . 8 8
  1 3 . 2 4
+ 1 0 . 9 4
  ─────────
  4 8 . 4 3
    2 2
```

Their total time for the race was 48.43 seconds.

PAGE 11 — SUBTRACTION

1.   E

You need to subtract 48.28 from 75.63.
Partition 48.28 into 40.00, 8.00, 0.20 and 0.08.
75.63 – 40.00 = 35.63
35.63 – 8.00 = 27.63
27.63 – 0.20 = 27.43
27.43 – 0.08 = 27.35

2.   Joe

You could count on in stages from each person's score in test 1 to their score in test 2 to work out their increase in test score:

Joe: 57.6 →0.4→ 58 →3→ 61 →0.5→ 61.5
0.4 + 3 + 0.5 = 3.9%

Lucille: 62.7 →0.3→ 63 →3→ 66 →0.4→ 66.4
0.3 + 3 + 0.4 = 3.7%

Anita: 59.8 →0.2→ 60 →3→ 63 →0.6→ 63.6
0.2 + 3 + 0.6 = 3.8%

So Joe had the greatest increase in score.
(Holly's and Dave's scores decreased between test 1 and test 2, so the answer can't be either of them.)

PAGES 12-13 — MULTIPLYING AND DIVIDING BY 10, 100 AND 1000

Warm-Up Activity
0.063, 0.63, 6.3, 63, 630, 6300

Compare the place value of each of the digits in the numbers to put them in the correct order.

1.   B

Start by working out how many books of tickets were sold. Divide the number of tickets sold by the number of tickets in a book: 1000 ÷ 10 = 100 books. Then divide the amount of money collected by the number of books sold to find the cost of each book: 375 ÷ 100 = £3.75.

2.   0.0042

4.2 ÷ 10 = 0.42. The number that fills in the blank should equal 0.42 when it's multiplied by 100. So, divide 0.42 by 100 to find the missing number. 0.42 ÷ 100 = 0.0042.

PAGE 16 — MULTIPLICATION

1.   27 650

350 is 100 times larger than 3.5. 79 is 10 times larger than 7.9. So, the answer to 350 × 79 will be 1000 (100 × 10) times larger than 27.65. 27.65 × 1000 = 27 650.

2. **A**

Round the cost of the toy robot up to £5.50, then multiply by 6.
You could partition £5.50 to make the multiplication easier:
£5.00 × 6 = £30.00
£0.50 × 6 = £3.00
£30.00 + £3.00 = £33.00
Then subtract the 6p that you rounded up by to get the answer:
£33.00 – £0.06 = £32.94

3. **D**

Estimate the answer by rounding each value to the nearest
whole number and then multiplying the rounded values together:
6.9 rounds up to 7, 8.2 rounds down to 8. 8 × 7 = 56, so the answer
is around 56. The only realistic option is option D, 56.58.

4. **954**

Use written multiplication to find the answer:

$$\begin{array}{r} 53 \\ \times \ 18 \\ \hline 424 \\ {}^2 \\ + \ 530 \\ \hline 954 \end{array}$$

PAGE 19 — DIVISION

1. **2.2**

First, convert the decimal into a whole number: 8.8 × 10 = 88.
Then do the division: 88 ÷ 4 = 22. Since you multiplied 8.8 by 10
at the beginning, you've got to divide your answer by 10 now.
22 ÷ 10 = 2.2.

2. **11**

You need to divide 14.50 by 1.30 to see how many lots of 1.30
there are in 14.50. Partition 14.50 into numbers that are easier to
work with. Find a number that's close to 14.50 and is a multiple of
1.30 — there are 10 lots of 1.30 in 13.00, which leaves you with
1.50 left over (14.50 – 13.00 = 1.50). This is enough to buy 1 more
soft toy (1.50 – 1.30 = 0.20). The total number of toys you can buy
is 10 + 1 = 11.

3. **C**

The answer to 19 200 ÷ 4 will be four times larger than the
answer to 19 200 ÷ 16 (because 4 is four times smaller than 16).
So, multiply 1200 by 4 to find the answer to 19 200 ÷ 4.
1200 × 4 = 4800.

4. **33**

You need to divide 264 by 8. Split 264 into two smaller numbers
that are easier to divide — e.g. 64 and 200.
64 ÷ 8 = 8
200 ÷ 8 = 25
Add the answers together to find the final answer:
8 + 25 = 33 levels

PAGE 21 — MIXED CALCULATIONS

1. **18**

Follow BODMAS to do the calculations in the correct order.
Do the bit in brackets first:
6 + 4 × 3² ÷ 3
Then work out the square number:
6 + 4 × 9 ÷ 3
Next work out the division:
6 + 4 × 3
Then work out the multiplication:
6 + 12
Finally do the addition:
6 + 12 = 18

2. **14 610**

1.7 and 8.3 are both multiplied by 1450. Add 1.7 and 8.3 together
and multiply the total by 1450:
1.7 + 8.3 = 10
10 × 1450 = 14 500
Then you need to add on 110:
14 500 + 110 = 14 610

SECTION TWO — NUMBER KNOWLEDGE

PAGE 23 — TYPES OF NUMBER

1. **19**

The person who works on the highest floor is Heather, on floor 15.
The person who works on the lowest floor is Archie, on floor -4.
To get from -4 to 0 you add 4. To get from 0 to 15 you add 15.
4 + 15 = 19

PAGE 26 — FACTORS, MULTIPLES AND PRIMES

1. **E**

A — false, 3 is a factor of 24 and is not a multiple of 2.
B — false, 13 is a common factor of 13 and 52.
C — false, not all numbers ending in 3 are multiples of 3, e.g. 13.
D — false, the highest common factor of 36 and 18 is 18.
E — true, 3 is a prime number and a multiple of 3.

2. **C**

72 can be divided exactly by 4, 6, 8 and 9.
72 ÷ 4 = 18, 72 ÷ 6 = 12, 72 ÷ 8 = 9, 72 ÷ 9 = 8.
But, 72 doesn't divide exactly by 7.

PAGE 29 — FRACTIONS

1. **E**

Lydia gave Gemma $\frac{2}{5}$ of her pie. So Lydia is left with $\frac{3}{5}$ of a pie.
Rose gave Gemma $\frac{1}{5}$ of her pie. So Rose is left with $\frac{4}{5}$ and Gemma
has $\frac{2}{5} + \frac{1}{5} = \frac{3}{5}$ of a pie. So Lydia and Gemma have the same
amount of pie.

2. **B**

Ilya and Alex have two bags of 6 apples, so the total number of apples
= 12. To find the number taken by each person you could divide 12 by
the denominator and then multiply the result by the numerator.
Ilya took $\frac{1}{4}$ of 12 apples: 12 ÷ 4 = 3, 3 × 1 = 3 apples.
Alex took $\frac{2}{3}$ of the apples: 12 ÷ 3 = 4, 4 × 2 = 8 apples.
Alex and Ilya took a total of 3 + 8 = 11 apples.
So the number left = 12 – 11 = 1.

PAGE 31 — RATIO AND PROPORTION

1. **1.2 orange cows to black and white cows**

First write the ratio out using the numbers in the question:
48:96
Next, simplify the ratio by dividing both sides by the same number.
Keep going until both sides can't be divided any more. For example:
Divide both 48 and 96 by 12 to give a ratio of 4:8
Divide both 4 and 8 by 4 to give a ratio of 1:2
1:2 can't be divided any more so the answer is in its simplest form.

2.   60

To find the number of green blocks, turn the ratio into a fraction — $\frac{5}{7}$.
Divide 84 by the denominator:
84 ÷ 7 = 12
Then multiply by the numerator:
12 × 5 = 60
Maya has 60 green blocks.

PAGE 34 — PERCENTAGES, FRACTIONS AND DECIMALS

1.   C

There are 8 triangles in this shape and 2 are shaded in, so that's $\frac{2}{8}$.
You can simplify this to $\frac{1}{4}$. $\frac{1}{4}$ is equal to 25%.

2.   B

Reading off the chart, 20% of children chose pink as their favourite
colour. 20% of 90 is the same as $\frac{2}{10}$ of 90. 90 ÷ 10 = 9.
9 × 2 = 18.

3.   A

A — 25% of 4 is the same as $\frac{1}{4}$ of 4. 4 ÷ 4 = 1. 1 × 1 = 1
B — $\frac{3}{4}$ of 8. 8 ÷ 4 = 2. 2 × 3 = 6.
C — $\frac{2}{5}$ of 10. 10 ÷ 5 = 2. 2 × 2 = 4.
D — 10% of 25 is the same as $\frac{1}{10}$ of 25.
*   25 ÷ 10 = 2.5. 2.5 × 1 = 2.5*
E — $\frac{2}{6}$ of 18. 18 ÷ 6 = 3. 3 × 2 = 6.
A is the smallest.

SECTION THREE — NUMBER PROBLEMS

PAGES 35-38 — ALGEBRA

Warm-Up Activity
8 × 6 = 48
62 − 19 = 43
8 × 5 = 40
84 ÷ 12 = 7
46 + 27 = 73
34 − 16 = 18

1.   £75

The number of hours is 3 and the cost of the parts is £20.
Put these values into the equation.
C = 25 + 10h + p
C = 25 + 10 × 3 + 20
C = 25 + 30 + 20
C = 75
The cost of the electrician is £75.

2.   64

Remove parts of the equation so that the x is left on its own.
x ÷ 8 − 6 = 2
First add 6 to both sides:
x ÷ 8 = 8
Then multiply both sides of the equation by 8:
x = 64
The value of x is 64.

3.   D

Work out each part of the algebraic expression:
The width of the room is 3 metres.
The length of the room is 4 × 3 = 12 metres
(4 times the width).
The height of the room is y metres.
To calculate the volume, multiply the width, length and
height together:
Volume = 3 × 12 × y = 36 y

PAGES 39-41 — NUMBER SEQUENCES

Warm-Up Activity
9 and 47

The difference between each number in the sequence is 9
(e.g. 2 + 9 = 11). The next number in the sequence is 38 + 9 = 47.

1.   39

The sequence is 4, 9, 15. The difference between the numbers is
increased by one each time. So the difference between 4 and 9 is 5,
and 9 and 15 is 6. To find the fourth number you'd add 7, to find the
fifth you'd add 8, and to find the sixth you'd add 9.
15 + 7 = 22. 22 + 8 = 30. 30 + 9 = 39.

2.   5n + 2

The sequence increases by 5 for each term, so you need to multiply by
5 in the expression — 5n. For the first term, if you multiply by 5 you
get 5 × 1 = 5. The actual number in the sequence is 7. Add 2 to your
expression to get a sequence that works for the first term — 5n + 2.
Test this to see if it works for the other terms:
2nd term: 5 × 2 + 2 = 12 — correct.
3rd term: 5 × 3 + 2 = 17 — correct
4th term: 5 × 4 + 2 = 22 — correct
5th term: 5 × 5 + 2 = 27 — correct

PAGE 45 — WORD PROBLEMS

1.   E

To get 42 tulips, Lena needs to buy 6 bunches of tulips (42 ÷ 7 = 6).
To get 42 roses, Lena needs to buy 7 bunches of roses (42 ÷ 6 = 7).
So 6 × 4.50 = £27, 7 × 3.50 = £24.50. 27 + 24.50 = £51.50

2.   £1.70

You need to work out how much Benni spent.
So £10 − £1.50 = £8.50.
This means that 5 sandwiches cost £8.50. The sandwiches all cost
the same so the cost of 1 sandwich is £8.50 ÷ 5 = £1.70

3.   £17.10

You could work out the profit that Simone makes on each bracelet.
50p − 20p = 30p. Then multiply this by the number she sells. The
easiest thing to do here is to round the number she sells (57) up to
an easier number (60), then do the multiplication. 30 × 60 can be
worked out by finding 3 × 6 = 18, then add on the two zeros to give
1800p, or £18.00. Because you rounded the number sold up by
three, you just need to subtract the cost of 3 bracelets
(3 × 30p = 90p) from £18.00 to give you the answer.
£18.00 − 90p = £17.10.

SECTION FOUR — DATA HANDLING

PAGE 47 — DATA TABLES

1.   B

The number of children who own more than 15 DVDs is shown by the frequencies in the bottom two rows of the table. Find the total number of children by adding these frequencies together: 13 + 6 = 19.

2.   £6

First find the total amount spent on senior citizen tickets by subtracting the cost of the adult tickets, child tickets and the booking fee from the "Amount to pay".
£212.50 – £2.50 – £32 – £160 = £18.
The table shows that three senior citizen tickets were bought, so divide £18 by 3 to find the cost of one ticket: £18 ÷ 3 = £6.

PAGE 51 — DISPLAYING DATA

1.   36

You know that 20° = 2 children, so 10° = 1 child. The whole pie chart is 360° and 360° ÷ 10 = 36, so there are 36 children in the class.

PAGE 53 — ANALYSING DATA

1.   21

Mean = (22 + 23 + 17 + 17 + 26) ÷ 5 = 105 ÷ 5 = 21.

PAGES 54-55 — MISLEADING DATA

Warm-Up Activity
The article claims that sprouts are more popular with girls than boys, but the data shows that the same proportion of boys and girls like sprouts.

The article says that 75% of boys don't like sprouts so that means that 100 – 75 = 25% of boys do like them. 25% is the same as $\frac{1}{4}$, so an equal proportion of boys and girls like sprouts. The article is misleading because it claims that sprouts are more popular with girls than boys.

1.   C

The headline suggests that sales of pencils have fallen by a massive amount. If you read the graph, the sales have only actually fallen from 500 million to 498 million. The graph makes it look like the sales have fallen more sharply because the axis doesn't start at zero — the drop isn't actually very big compared to the overall number of pencils sold.

SECTION FIVE — SHAPE AND SPACE

PAGE 57 — ANGLES

1.   D

Angle c is smaller than a right angle, so it is less than 90°. This means that it must be either 10° or 45°. You can tell that it is about half of the size of a right angle, so the correct answer is option D — 45°.

2.   135°

The total size of the angles on the circular compass is 360°. There are 8 compass points, so the size of the angle between each point is 360 ÷ 8 = 45°. South is three points away from north east so the size of the angle between them is 45 × 3 = 135°.

PAGE 61 — 2D SHAPES

1.   C

The shape has no right angles so it can't be a right-angled triangle. It has no equal sides so it can't be equilateral or isosceles. All the sides and angles in a scalene triangle are different — so the answer is option C.

2.   A

First, rule out the shapes that can't go in that row. A square, an equilateral triangle and a rhombus have all equal side lengths, so you can rule out B, D and E. Next, rule out the shapes that can't go in that column. A rectangle has all equal angles, so you can rule out C. The answer must be A — a trapezium.

3.   Isosceles triangle

The shape has no obtuse angles, so all the angles inside the shape must be 90° or less — this means the shape can only be a square, a rectangle or a triangle. The next clue says that it has no right angles, so it can't be a square or a rectangle — it must be a triangle. The final clue says that two of its sides are equal in length. A right-angled triangle or an isosceles triangle can have two equal side lengths, but this shape doesn't have any right angles. The shape is an isosceles triangle.

PAGE 65 — 2D SHAPES – PERIMETER AND AREA

1.   7.5 cm

The perimeter of the shape is made up of 10 equal length sides. The length of each side is 75 ÷ 10 = 7.5 cm. So, side Z is 7.5 cm.

2.   C

Split the shape into two rectangles as shown in the diagram. Work out the length of the missing sides on the smaller rectangle. The horizontal side is 13 – 5 – 5 = 3 cm and the vertical side is 8 – 4 = 4 cm.

Then work out the area of each rectangle. The smaller rectangle is 3 × 4 = 12 cm². The larger rectangle is 13 × 4 = 52 cm². The total area of the shape is 52 + 12 = 64 cm² — option C is correct.

PAGE 67 — SYMMETRY

1.   A

The shape is a trapezium.
The diagram shows the reflected shape.

2.   5

The star has 5 lines of symmetry. These are shown on the diagram.

PAGE 71 — 3D SHAPES

1.   B

Option B is the only net that will not fold up to make a cube — two of its faces would overlap. The diagram below shows which faces would overlap if you folded it up.

2.   64

The number of vegetable stock cubes that will fit along the length of the box is 4 cm ÷ 1 cm = 4. The number that will fit along the width of the box is 8 cm ÷ 1 cm = 8. The number that will fit up the height of the box is 2 cm ÷ 1 cm = 2. The total number of cubes is 4 × 8 × 2 = 64 vegetable stock cubes.

3.   Cuboid

The net has 4 rectangular faces in a line, then 2 squares at the top and bottom — it will fold up to make a cuboid. (A cuboid can also be called a rectangular prism.)

PAGE 74 — SHAPE PROBLEMS

1.   C

When you look at the logo from the back of the window it will be flipped over horizontally, so you need to look for the option that's a reflection of the original logo. Option C is a reflection of the original logo.

PAGE 76 — COORDINATES

1.   D

Go through the options one by one. Imagine plotting each of the points on the grid. A parallelogram is a shape with two pairs of equal length, parallel sides, a pair of equal obtuse angles and a pair of equal acute angles. Only the coordinates for option D make a parallelogram with the existing points on the grid.

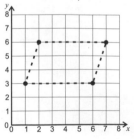

2.   (4, 4)

Read off the coordinates of the campsite (7, 7) and the car park (1, 1). Halfway between the two x-axis coordinates (1 and 7) is 4. Halfway between the two y-axis coordinates (1 and 7) is also 4. So the coordinates of the farmhouse are (4, 4).

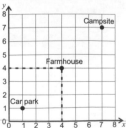

PAGE 78 — TRANSFORMATIONS

1.   (6, 4)

The diagram shows the shape after it has been reflected in the mirror line. The coordinates of corner Y are now (6, 4).

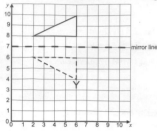

2.   (–1, 4)

Read off the original coordinates of point Z (5, 7). The new coordinates will have an x value that is 6 less than the original x coordinate (5 – 6 = –1), and a y value that is 3 less than the original y coordinate (7 – 3 = 4). The new coordinates of point Z are (–1, 4).

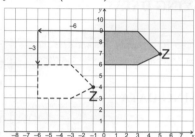

SECTION SIX — UNITS AND MEASURES

PAGE 81 — UNITS

1.   D

0.3 g, 3 g and 30 g are all very light — less than the weight of an empty schoolbag, so the answer can't be any of these options. 30 kg is very heavy — about the weight of a child, so this can't be the answer either. The answer must be 3 kg — this is about the weight of 3 bags of sugar, which could easily be carried.

2.   71 servings

There is originally 28.75 litres = 28 750 ml of soup (28.75 × 1000). 350 ml is spilt, so there is 28 750 – 350 = 28 400 ml left. Now you need to divide 28 400 ml by 400 ml to find the number of servings. To simplify the calculation, you could divide both numbers by 100: 28400 ÷ 400 = 284 ÷ 4. Now use a written method to do the division: $4\overline{)2\,{}^2 8\,4}$ = 71

3.   A

Each stride is 50 cm so 2 strides will cover 2 × 50 cm = 100 cm. There are 100 cm in 1 m, so Ben takes 2 strides to walk 1 m. There are 1000 m in 1 km, so in 10 km there are 10 × 1000 = 10 000 m. So to walk 10 000 m Ben must take 10 000 × 2 = 20 000 strides.

PAGE 84 — TIME

1.   Max

The youngest child must have the latest date of birth. Children born in 2009 must be younger than those born in 2008, so it can't be Jim or Geeta. October is later in 2009 than March and May, so Max must be younger than Meg and Fred.

2.   February

Keep adding the number of pages Kerry completes each month until you reach 154.
Sep = 30
Sep + Oct = 30 + 31 = 61
Sep + Oct + Nov = 61 + 30 = 91
Sep + Oct + Nov + Dec = 91 + 31 = 122
Sep + Oct + Nov + Dec + Jan = 122 + 31 = 153
There are 153 days between September and the end of January,
so she will finish her 154-page book in February.

3.   D

Work out the time difference in stages like this:

Total = 7 mins + 2 hours + 15 mins = 2 hours 22 minutes
Watch out — this isn't the same as 2.22 hours.
2.22 hours is 2 hours and 22 hundredths of an hour.

SECTION SEVEN — MIXED PROBLEMS

PAGES 85-88 — MIXED PROBLEMS

Warm-Up Activity
10% of 40 = ¼ of 16
10% of 40 = 40 ÷ 10 = 4, ¼ of 16 = 16 ÷ 4 = 4
5^2 – 10 = 3 × 5
5^2 – 10 = 25 – 10 = 15, 3 × 5 = 15
(5 + 3) × 7 = 30 + 26
(5 + 3) × 7 = 8 × 7 = 56, 30 + 26 = 56
0.73 × 100 = 54 + 19
0.73 × 100 = 73, 54 + 19 = 73

1.   £40

Work out the volume of the swimming pool.
10 × 10 × 1.6 = 160 m^3.
If it costs 25p to fill 1 m^3 then it will cost £1 to fill 4 m^3.
160 ÷ 4 = 40, so it will cost £40 in total.

2.   B

The pie chart is a circle so all of the angles add up to 360°.
A section that is 90° would cover $\frac{1}{4}$ (or 25%) of the pie chart
(360 ÷ 4 = 90°). The section for red flowers covers 45° which is half
of 90°. So as a percentage, 45° is 25% ÷ 2 = 12.5%. The correct
answer is option B.

Index

MHRDE1

SECTION FOUR — DATA HANDLING

PAGE 47 — DATA TABLES

1.   B

The number of children who own more than 15 DVDs is shown by the frequencies in the bottom two rows of the table. Find the total number of children by adding these frequencies together: 13 + 6 = 19.

2.   £6

First find the total amount spent on senior citizen tickets by subtracting the cost of the adult tickets, child tickets and the booking fee from the "Amount to pay".
£212.50 – £2.50 – £32 – £160 = £18.
The table shows that three senior citizen tickets were bought, so divide £18 by 3 to find the cost of one ticket: £18 ÷ 3 = £6.

PAGE 51 — DISPLAYING DATA

1.   36

You know that 20° = 2 children, so 10° = 1 child. The whole pie chart is 360° and 360° ÷ 10 = 36, so there are 36 children in the class.

PAGE 53 — MODE, MEDIAN, MEAN AND RANGE

1.   B

Work out the mean, mode, median and range for the data set you're given.
Mean = (22 + 23 + 17 + 17 + 26) ÷ 5 = 105 ÷ 5 = 21.
Mode = most common value = 17
The number of tea bags listed from smallest to largest:
17 17 22 23 26
Median = middle value = 22
Range = 26 – 17 = 9
Compare your values to the options — B is the correct option.

PAGES 54-55 — MISLEADING DATA

Warm-Up Activity
The article claims that sprouts are more popular with girls than boys, but the data shows that the same proportion of boys and girls like sprouts.

The article says that 75% of boys don't like sprouts so that means that 100 – 75 = 25% of boys do like them. 25% is the same as ¼, so an equal proportion of boys and girls like sprouts. The article is misleading because it claims that sprouts are more popular with girls than boys.

1.   C

The headline suggests that sales of pencils have fallen by a massive amount. If you read the graph, the sales have only actually fallen from 500 million to 498 million. The graph makes it look like the sales have fallen more sharply because the axis doesn't start at zero — the drop isn't actually very big compared to the overall number of pencils sold.

PAGE 57 — PROBABILITY

1.   C

Go through the options and see if they're true:
A — There is a total of 6 + 3 = 9 in the 'Girl' circle, and only 2 + 5 = 7 outside the girl circle — there are more girls than boys, so not an even chance.
B — There are 2 + 3 = 5 glasses wearers, and 6 + 3 + 2 + 5 = 16 children in total. 5 isn't one quarter of 16, so this statement isn't true.
C — Boy glasses-wearers are shown in the 'Glasses-wearer' circle, but outside of the 'Girl' circle. There are 2 of them, which as a fraction of the total is ²⁄₁₆. If you divide both the numerator and denominator by 2, this simplifies to ⅛. So this statement is true.
D — There are 3 + 2 = 5 glasses-wearers out of 16, so there is less chance that the child selected will be a glasses-wearer than not.
E — There are 3 girls who wear glasses (shown by the overlap of the circles). 3 out of 16 isn't equal to 50%.

SECTION FIVE — SHAPE AND SPACE

PAGE 59 — ANGLES

1.   D

Angle c is smaller than a right angle, so it is less than 90°. This means that it must be either 10° or 45°. You can tell that it is about half of the size of a right angle, so the correct answer is option D — 45°.

2.   135°

The total size of the angles on the circular compass is 360°. There are 8 compass points, so the size of the angle between each point is 360° ÷ 8 = 45°. South is three points away from north east so the size of the angle between them is 45 × 3 = 135°.

PAGE 63 — 2D SHAPES

1.   C

The shape has no right angles so it can't be a right-angled triangle. It has no equal sides so it can't be equilateral or isosceles. All the sides and angles in a scalene triangle are different — so the answer is option C.

2.   A

First, rule out the shapes that can't go in that row. A square, an equilateral triangle and a rhombus have all equal side lengths, so you can rule out B, D and E. Next, rule out the shapes that can't go in that column. A rectangle has all equal angles, so you can rule out C. The answer must be A — a trapezium.

3.   Isosceles triangle

The shape has no obtuse angles, so all the angles inside the shape must be 90° or less — this means the shape can only be a square, a rectangle or a triangle. The next clue says that it has no right angles, so it can't be a square or a rectangle — it must be a triangle. The final clue says that two of its sides are equal in length. A right-angled triangle or an isosceles triangle can have two equal side lengths, but this shape doesn't have any right angles. The shape is an isosceles triangle.

PAGE 67 — 2D SHAPES – PERIMETER AND AREA

1.   7.5 cm

The perimeter of the shape is made up of 10 equal length sides. The length of each side is 75 ÷ 10 = 7.5 cm. So, side Z is 7.5 cm.

2.   C

Split the shape into two rectangles as shown in the diagram. Work out the length of the missing sides on the smaller rectangle. The horizontal side is 13 – 5 – 5 = 3 cm and the vertical side is 8 – 4 = 4 cm.

Then work out the area of each rectangle. The smaller rectangle is 3 × 4 = 12 cm². The larger rectangle is 13 × 4 = 52 cm². The total area of the shape is 52 + 12 = 64 cm² — option C is correct.

PAGE 70 — SYMMETRY

1.   A

The shape is a trapezium. The diagram shows the reflected shape.

2.   5

The star has 5 lines of symmetry. These are shown on the diagram.

3.   5

You need to imagine the shape being rotated in your head. Each time the points of the star rotate around to where one of the other points was, the shape will look exactly the same. The star has 5 points, so it will have an order of rotational symmetry of 5.

PAGE 74 — 3D SHAPES

1.   B

Option B is the only net that will not fold up to make a cube — two of its faces would overlap. The diagram below shows which faces would overlap if you folded it up.

2.   64

The number of vegetable stock cubes that will fit along the length of the box is 4 cm ÷ 1 cm = 4. The number that will fit along the width of the box is 8 cm ÷ 1 cm = 8. The number that will fit up the height of the box is 2 cm ÷ 1 cm = 2. The total number of cubes is 4 × 8 × 2 = 64 vegetable stock cubes.

3.   Cuboid

The net has 4 rectangular faces in a line, then 2 squares at the top and bottom — it will fold up to make a cuboid. (A cuboid can also be called a rectangular prism.)

PAGE 77 — SHAPE PROBLEMS

1.   C

When you look at the logo from the back of the window it will be flipped over horizontally, so you need to look for the option that's a reflection of the original logo. Option C is a reflection of the original logo.

PAGE 79 — COORDINATES

1.   D

Go through the options one by one. Imagine plotting each of the points on the grid. A parallelogram is a shape with two pairs of equal length, parallel sides, a pair of equal obtuse angles and a pair of equal acute angles. Only the coordinates for option D make a parallelogram with the existing points on the grid.

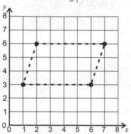

2.   (4, 4)

Read off the coordinates of the campsite (7, 7) and the car park (1, 1). Halfway between the two x-axis coordinates (1 and 7) is 4. Halfway between the two y-axis coordinates (1 and 7) is also 4. So the coordinates of the farmhouse are (4, 4).

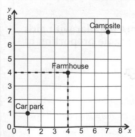

PAGE 81 — TRANSFORMATIONS

1.   (5, 3)

The diagram shows the shape after it has been rotated 90° anticlockwise about the point (6, 7). The coordinates of corner Y are now (5, 3).

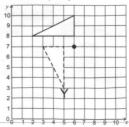

2.   (–1, 4)

Read off the original coordinates of point Z (5, 7). The new coordinates will have an x value that is 6 less than the original x coordinate (5 – 6 = –1), and a y value that is 3 less than the original y coordinate (7 – 3 = 4). The new coordinates of point Z are (–1, 4).

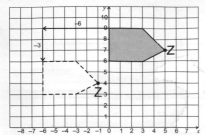

SECTION SIX — UNITS AND MEASURES

PAGE 84 — UNITS

1.   D

0.3 g, 3 g and 30 g are all very light — less than the weight of an empty schoolbag, so the answer can't be any of these options.
30 kg is very heavy — about the weight of a child, so this can't be the answer either. The answer must be 3 kg — this is about the weight of 3 bags of sugar, which could easily be carried.

2.   71 servings

There is originally 28.75 litres = 28 750 ml of soup (28.75 × 1000). 350 ml is spilt, so there is 28 750 – 350 = 28 400 ml left.
Now you need to divide 28 400 ml by 400 ml to find the number of servings. To simplify the calculation, you could divide both numbers by 100: 28400 ÷ 400 = 284 ÷ 4.
Now use a written method to do the division: $4\overline{)2\,^2 8\,^2 4}$ = 71

3.   A

Each stride is 50 cm so 2 strides will cover 2 × 50 cm = 100 cm. There are 100 cm in 1 m, so Ben takes 2 strides to walk 1 m. There are 1000 m in 1 km, so in 10 km there are 10 × 1000 = 10 000 m. So to walk 10 000 m Ben must take 10 000 × 2 = 20 000 strides.

PAGE 87 — TIME

1.   Max

The youngest child must have the latest date of birth. Children born in 2009 must be younger than those born in 2008, so it can't be Jim or Geeta. October is later in 2009 than March and May, so Max must be younger than Meg and Fred.

2.   February

Keep adding the number of pages Kerry completes each month until you reach 154.
Sep = 30
Sep + Oct = 30 + 31 = 61
Sep + Oct + Nov = 61 + 30 = 91
Sep + Oct + Nov + Dec = 91 + 31 = 122
Sep + Oct + Nov + Dec + Jan = 122 + 31 = 153
There are 153 days between September and the end of January, so she will finish her 154-page book in February.

3.   D

Work out the time difference in stages like this:

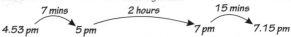

Total = 7 mins + 2 hours + 15 mins = 2 hours 22 minutes
Watch out — this isn't the same as 2.22 hours.
2.22 hours is 2 hours and 22 hundredths of an hour.

SECTION SEVEN — MIXED PROBLEMS

PAGES 88-91 — MIXED PROBLEMS

Warm-Up Activity
10% of 40 = ¼ of 16
10% of 40 = 40 ÷ 10 = 4, ¼ of 16 = 16 ÷ 4 = 4
5² – 10 = 3 × 5
5² – 10 = 25 – 10 = 15, 3 × 5 = 15
(5 + 3) × 7 = 30 + 26
(5 + 3) × 7 = 8 × 7 = 56, 30 + 26 = 56
0.73 × 100 = 54 + 19
0.73 × 100 = 73, 54 + 19 = 73

1.   £40

Work out the volume of the swimming pool.
10 × 10 × 1.6 = 160 m³.
If it costs 25p to fill 1 m³ then it will cost £1 to fill 4 m³.
160 ÷ 4 = 40, so it will cost £40 in total.

2.   B

The pie chart is a circle so all of the angles add up to 360°. A section that is 90° would cover ¼ (or 25%) of the pie chart (360 ÷ 4 = 90°). The section for red flowers covers 45° which is half of 90°. So as a percentage, 45° is 25% ÷ 2 = 12.5%. The correct answer is option B.

Index

MHRDE1